Educational Injustices among Margins and Centers

Studies in Criticality

Shirley R. Steinberg
General Editor
Vol. 546

Educational Injustices among Margins and Centers

Theorizing Critical Futures in Education

Edited by
Phillip A. Boda

PETER LANG
Lausanne - Berlin - Bruxelles - Chennai - New York - Oxford

Library of Congress Cataloging-in-Publication Data

Names: Boda, Phillip A., editor.
Title: Educational injustices among margins and centers : theorizing critical futures in education / edited by Phillip A. Boda.
Description: New York : Peter Lang, 2024. | Series: Counterpoints, 1058-1634 ; Vol. 546 | Includes bibliographical references.
Identifiers: LCCN 2023036333 (print) | LCCN 2023036334 (ebook) | ISBN 9781433199608 (paperback) | ISBN 9781433199592 (hardback) | ISBN 9781433197185 (pdf) | ISBN 9781433197192 (epub)
Subjects: LCSH: Educational sociology. | Discrimination in education. | Educational equalization. | Marginality, Social.
Classification: LCC LC191 .E4269 2024 (print) | LCC LC191 (ebook) | DDC 379.2/6–dc23/eng/20230913
LC record available at https://lccn.loc.gov/2023036333
LC ebook record available at https://lccn.loc.gov/2023036334
DOI 10.3726/b21223

Bibliographic information published by the Deutsche Nationalbibliothek.
The German National Library lists this publication in the German National Bibliography; detailed bibliographic data is available on the Internet at http://dnb.d-nb.de

Cover design by Peter Lang Group AG

ISSN 1058-1634
ISBN 9781433199592 (hardback)
ISBN 9781433199608 (paperback)
ISBN 9781433197185 (ebook)
ISBN 9781433197192 (epub)
DOI 10.3726/b21223

© 2024 Peter Lang Group AG, Lausanne
Published by Peter Lang Publishing Inc., New York, USA
info@peterlang.com - www.peterlang.com

All rights reserved.
All parts of this publication are protected by copyright.
Any utilization outside the strict limits of the copyright law, without the permission of the publisher, is forbidden and liable to prosecution.
This applies in particular to reproductions, translations, microfilming, and storage and processing in electronic retrieval systems.

This publication has been peer reviewed.

I dedicate this volume to all the peoples around the world that fall prey, by design, to the global capitalist agenda that seeks to erase any and all humanities that aren't profitable and exploitative. We see you; we hear you; we love you: **Your Lives-Hopes-Dreams Matter.**

CONTENTS

	List of Illustrations and Tables	ix
	Introduction *Phillip A. Boda*	1
1.	Wondering in the Dark *Monét Cooper*	7
2.	Honoring Homeplace: Centering Youth and Community Scholars as Co-constructors of Curriculum and Research *Miranda Goosby, Valentina Gamboa-Turner, and Erica R. Dávila*	13
3.	Engaging a Radical Poetics of Healing by Design: On Poiesis, Disobedience, and the Pursuit of Liberated Selves *Phillip A. Boda*	25

CONTENTS

4. Becoming LBS: Exploring Ambitions and Tensions in (De)constructing a Humanizing Undergraduate Teacher Preparation Program 39
   Laurie Inman and Jen Stacy

5. Belonging Despite Borders: An Autoethnographic Response to U.S. Imperialism, Migration, and Identity 43
   Van Anh Tran and M. Yianella Blanco

6. Fractional Crystallization as a Metaphor for a Palimpsest of Colonization 59
   Meghan Zarnetske

7. Neither Here Nor There: Graduate Students Navigating the Complexities of Motherscholarship During COVID-19 71
   Maureen W. Nicol and Abby C. Emerson

8. Inextricably Bound: Racialized Blackness and (Il)literacy in the United States' Imaginary 77
   CoCo Massengale

9. How Can I Teach Antiracism in My All-White Classroom? A Call to White Teachers 97
   Julia Kingsdale, Scout Cohen-Pope, and Cynthia Benally

10. "But Look at My Sign!" We Cried: And Other Types of White Performance That Will Never Dismantle the House 113
    Scott D. Farver

11. The Crip Futures of Academic Madness: Education, Schooling, and the Struggle Against Sanism 123
    Sam Shelton

12. The Hegemony in the Room 135
    Phillip A. Boda

LIST OF ILLUSTRATIONS AND TABLES

Figure 7.1. Mothering, working, nursing, sleeping (barely). 73
Figure 7.2. Mothering, commenting, bathing, caring. 74
Table 9.1. Literature Reviewed, Including Participants and Settings 100

INTRODUCTION
Phillip A. Boda

> Our living depends on our ability to conceptualize alternatives ... Colonialization made of us the colonized—participants in daily rituals of power where we, in strict sado-masochistic fashion, find pleasure in ways of being and thinking, ways of looking at the world that reinforce and maintain our positions as the dominated ... [and, in return for this obedience,] **one of the deepest expressions of our internalization of the colonizer's mentality has been self-censorship.**
> —hooks, 1990, pp. 149, 155, 157, bolding added

As the eminent bell hooks explains above, Living as a historically marginalized person in the world is both an act of resistance, as well as comes with a haunting of the colonial artifacts left over as the Western white European nations slaughtered, razed, and pillaged the lands of all people around the world, but most impactfully, Black, Brown, and Indigenous peoples. To "conceptualize alternatives," then, is the act of resistance when colonized peoples around the world (re)cognize and bear witness to the cultural hegemony that has been used for centuries in ways that can only be described as oppressive, tortuous, and downright murderous. And even then, as we witness this hegemony push forward ways of knowing and being that are in direct opposition to how peoples of the world have come to know themselves and their environment, we find institutions, such as schools in the West, where cultural domination and hegemony used to support repressive and ideological state apparatuses like the military and prison industrial complexes, there continue purposeful designs to uphold whiteness, heterosexism, ableism, and imperialism. They thereby become necessary factors used to exploit those peoples that have been historically marginalized even further, such as Trans Queer Black and Brown Disabled Peoples, where the goal is to strip them of their Lives-Hopes-Dreams, replacing their Futures with pathways and patterns of knowing that lead to contributing more power for the global capitalist project of Modernity where humans are valued for what they can produce, sell, and/or buy.

In turn, this volume is, first and foremost, a coalition-building work of love—radical, self-empowering Love (hooks, 2001). Moreover, given that "the primary responsibility for defining one's own reality lies with the people who live that reality" (Collins, 1991, p. 34), this volume sought out proposals that deconstruct structures and subjectivities, doing so by honoring authorship with and for those whose lived realities are discussed, authentically valuing and interweaving their experiences—who, then, "write all the things *they should have been able to read*," paraphrasing Collins (1991). Such workings, thus, also reconstructed new narratives of transformative futures that may not have answers right now. Following in the tradition of critical pedagogy, walkways of change that go together with rituals of questioning (*conocimiento*; Anzaldúa, 1987), and the charge for all educators with the "preparation of critical political subjects" (Giroux, 1993, p. 376), work that pushed the boundaries of what we have defined as equity, social justice, and liberation in schools and schooling were elicited. The submissions that were accepted, revised based on the Editorial Board's feedback (listed below), and included here constitute radical departures from what we have previously assumed are the margins and centers.

Chapter 1, *Wondering in the Dark* by monét cooper, for example, starts this volume speaking with and through a Black fugitivity and relational poetics to bring light where there was once darkness, and in turn also interrogate the understanding of darkness related to Blackness through a deconstructive and reconstructive analysis of Self and Other. Chapter 2, *Honoring Homeplace: Centering Youth and Community Scholars as Co-constructors of Curriculum and Research*, by Miranda Goosby, Valentina Gamboa-Turner, and Erica R. Dávila, similarly, engage the reader to think about the pragmatics of transforming schools and Selves in ways that work toward more just futures for all by developing a sharpened focus on healing during the learning process for teachers, community members, admin, and youth. Chapter 3, *Engaging a Radical Poetics of Healing by Design: On Poiesis, Disobedience, and the Pursuit of Liberated Selves*, by Phillip A. Boda, then transverses these two beginning texts to dive deeply into what we think we mean in relation Healing as an act of disobedience to the status quo of society that stands merely to stratify, categorize, segregate, and establish hierarchies to, by design, harm.

Lurking beyond these first three pieces, Chapter 4, *Becoming LBS: Exploring Ambitions and Tensions in (De)Constructing a Humanizing Undergraduate Teacher Preparation Program*, by Laurie Inman and Jen Stacy, bring us back to the entities that are needed engagement as teacher educators think about how to support the next generation of humanistic-trained teachers wherein they embody the nature of humanization as a tentative and always changing process. Chapter 5, *Belonging Despite Borders: An Autoethnographic Response to U.S. Imperialism, Migration, and Identity*, by Van Anh Tran and M. Yianella

Blanco, asks the reader then to take up the notion of transformative education beyond the halls of academia and of schooling spaces to interrogate how international powers and geopolitics play a role in understanding how our collective journey as critical pedagogues requires bearing witness to the intergenerational and diasporic ways that refugee and immigrant people come to know their positionality in education. Chapter 6, *Fractional Crystallization as a Metaphor for a Palimpsest of Colonization*, by Meghan Zarnetske, reinscribes the notions of complexity illustrated by the previous chapters in relation to coloniality and how analogies to neo-colonialization processes in education have played out in ways that provide venues to engage with our geo-historical and bio-political selves. Through these works, Self and Other are trouble with attention paid to their creation and praxis.

Chapter 7, *Neither Here Nor There: Graduate Students Navigating the Complexities of Motherscholarship During COVID-19*, by Maureen W. Nicol and Abby C. Emerson, emerges thereafter as a testimonio of being mother and graduate student as a transformative experience. The experiences of these motherscholars, which often involve balancing parenting with academics, are seen as a hindrance by institutions where these authors study, work, teach, and exist. However, they argue that by engaging in research, writing, and reading while parenting, scholars can challenge traditional roles and challenge patriarchal assumptions to bring new insights to educational research. In Chapter 8, *Inextricably Bound: Racialized Blackness and (Il)literacy in the United States' Imaginary*, by CoCo Massengale, she discusses the connection between being Black and being illiterate in the United States by examining how this relationship has been reinforced throughout history, beginning with the trans-Atlantic slave trade. CoCo goes on to explore how current discussions about Black people's reading abilities are connected to the past and identifies three main fears that influence these discussions: low achievement, association with crime, and economic cost; suggesting that there may be alternative ways of thinking about literacy and communication that could have a broader impact on society. Indeed, in Chapter 9, *How Can I Teach Antiracism in My All-White Classroom? A Call to White Teachers*, Julia Kingsdale, Scout Cohen-Pope, and Cynthia Benally examine how antiracist teaching practices are implemented in predominantly white K-12 classrooms, illuminating that there is a lack of research in this area, but that teacher choices are crucial to antiracist pedagogy, including asking questions, exposing and challenging whiteness in the classroom, and using texts strategically. They contend that to effectively use antiracist pedagogies, teachers need to understand whiteness, race, and racism, and base their practices on antiracist theory, especially in predominantly white classrooms. These three pieces coalesce a critical narrative beyond borders.

The last three contributions to this volume, Chapters 10–12, bring forth our radical imaginations about what is possible if we stand up to majority opinion, culture, ideology, and epistemology. Chapter 10, *"bUt LoOk aT My sIgN!" We Cried: And Other Types of White Performance That Will Never Dismantle the House*, by Scott D. Farver, begins this deep excavation process of understanding where white racial justice advocates' rhetoric and propaganda used in education. The poem discusses the concept of white "slacktivism," or publicly performing as an antiracist without taking any concrete action, especially through low-effort or low-cost means such as social media. The author uses his own experiences working with white future teachers to highlight how such performative "allyship" often falls short of the direct action and co-conspiracy. Chapter 11, *The Crip Futures of Academic Madness: Education, Schooling, and the Struggle Against Sanism*, by Sam Shelton, pushes up beyond our comfort zones and takes up the legibility of the Disabled standpoint, body, mind, and spirit to confront the sanism in education. Discussing the connections between education and the system of oppression known as "sanism," Shelton describes how this positioning discriminates against people with mental illnesses and argues that in order to work toward Mad liberation and more inclusive education for all, we need to fundamentally transform our understanding and practice of education. This includes challenging harmful ideas and norms that contribute to the oppression of people with mental illnesses with the goal to add a perspective based on lived experiences of violence and harm to the conversation about social justice education. Book-ending this volume, Chapter 12, *The Hegemony in the Room*, by Phillip A. Boda, leaves the reader with not a destination or set of benchmarks, but a relational and iteratively changed approach to understanding Self, Other, power, and authority via the lived realities of youth, adults, and other educational stakeholders—theorizing a praxis of resistance through Self.

Editorial Review Board

Dr. Wayne Au	University of Washington, Bothell
Dr. Patricia Baquedano-López	University of California, Berkeley
Dr. Phillip A. Boda	University of Illinois, Chicago

Dr. Sherice Clarke — University of California, San Diego
Dr. Danielle Cowley — Alfred University
Dr. AnaLouise Keating — Texas Woman's University
Dr. David Hernández-Saca — University of Northern Iowa
Dr. Shakhnoza Kayumova — University of Massachusetts, Dartmouth
Dr. Lauren Leigh Kelly — Rutgers, the State University of New Jersey
Dr. Natalie King — Georgia State University
Dr. Emily A. Nusbaum — Mills College and University of San Diego
Dr. Yolanda Sealey-Ruiz — Teachers College, Columbia University
Dr. Lisette Torres-Gerald — TERC
Dr. Chezare A. Warren — Michigan State University

References

Anzaldúa, G. (1987). *Borderlands/La Frontera: The new mestiza.* Aunt Lute Book Company.

Collins, P. H. (1991). *Black feminist thought: Knowledge, consciousness, and the politics of empowerment.* Routledge.

Freire, P. (1970). *Pedagogy of the oppressed* (M. B. Ramos, Trans.). Continuum.

Giroux, H. (1993). Literacy and the politics of difference. In C. Lankshear and P. L. McLaren (Eds.), *Critical literacy: Politics, praxis, and the postmodern* (pp. 367–377). SUNY Press.

hooks, b. (1990). *Yearning: Race, gender, and cultural politics.* South End Press.

hooks, b. (2001). *All about love: New visions.* Harper Perennial.

Schalk, S. (2011). Self, other and other-self: Going beyond the self/other binary in contemporary consciousness. *Journal of Comparative Research in Anthropology and Sociology, 2,* 197–210.

· 1 ·

WONDERING IN THE DARK

Monét Cooper

"Survival is a promise ... It is a promise I make in honor of the deaths that make this clarity not only possible, but unavoidable."
—Alexis Pauline Gumbs, *The Shape of My Impact*

"Our impact on this country, whether it is recognized or not, is where mattering rests; it is where thriving rests. Mattering is civics because it is the quest for humanity."
—Bettina Love, *We Want to Do More Than Survive: Abolitionist Teaching and the Pursuit of Educational Freedom*

back

after A. Van Jordan

1. (noun) **a.** *the rear surface of the human body from the shoulders to the hips:* (a) As in, the first time I kissed her, we were in high school. I licked my lips, put my arms around her shoulders and slowly kissed her cheek, neck and *back*. (b) She was laying in the backyard. When I walked to her body, she lay on her *back*. I saw her face first, then the lips that can't kiss me back. **b.** *the side or part of something that is away from the spectator or from the direction in which it moves or faces:* Swore she could play basketball like Jordan, but once we were out *back*, I beat her three times, easy. "One more," she smiled. Rolling up her shirt, she flew the ball, moving my ego through her fingers into air. Our feet began to dance, bodies parallel to the rock. She flung the ball against my broken concrete. Her smile soared into a laugh sung impolite as the day's sun, sweating us out

of our do-rags and pride. She took the ball from me as if I had passed it to her. Or, the ball knew she was home. I lost that last game we played. I remember, me, always at the *back* of her neck, us, feeling the other's heat, the ball jumping within reach. **c.** *the rear*: (a) Our teacher tried to seat her in the *back* of the class, but she said, "Nah, I want a seat in the front." Before Mr. W could respond, she sat in the seat she wanted, returning Mr. W's gaze. Later she told me, "Someone would sit in the *back*, but it didn't have to be no one in the room." (b) The news says the police shot her hugging her baby in the *back*. Truer: A month ago, we sat on my porch, her braiding my hair, predicting our future before dinner. We'd finish school. We'd love our children. We'd play as much ball as we could. Finish our hoop dreams. We'd be happy. We had a life. **d.** *the part of the body which bears burdens*: 2020. Also known as if I could touch the top of the pine trees between our houses, I would with both hands, but I'll settle for her eyes, the summer heat she told jokes in, her loudness, anger that cools itself upon arrival, right now her jersey number tatted on my heart and *back*.

2. (adverb) **a.** *toward the rear; in the opposite direction from the one that one is facing or traveling*. People said that when the final bullet went through her chest, she fell *back*. **b.** *expressing a return to an earlier or normal condition*: They asked me what the last thing I remember about her was: seeing her sprint to the back of the ice cream line at school, never thinking that she would not be coming *back*. I asked her mama and daddy what I could do. Mama J looked at her open palms, "How do you think we can bring my daughter *back*?" **c.** *into the past*: Her mama told me yesterday, "When I look *back*, after she left my womb, no sound or scream until the nurses took her from me, whispering and moving their hands across her still, little body. A gurgle, then my baby yelling. I looked at her as quiet filled their arms, then mine. Eyes open. We looked at each other. She's been here before, but I remember when she came back." **d.** *cover the back of (an object) in order to support, protect, or decorate it*: The police *back* each other's accounts. What I know of love is all truth, not like these stories they told about her on the news as if ain't no one love her *back*.

3. (adjective) *of or at the back of something*: Here she is, look at this photo on my timeline. There JoJo is behind Tamir and Brayla, they all smiling *back*.

Why I Teach

I.
I call the mother who adopted her
happy to report, ma'am,
your daughter is brilliant as stars
we see in daylight.

She exists
in my gradebook and beyond it.
An exponential
burst of light,
lean and rare.

Her smallness glints at the dissonance
awaiting her, she stares back
for she takes her life's confusions,
then organizes her essays out of it.

At 13, she has passed through needles' eyes,
countless times through her mother's legs,
more through those of whomever
mother brought to their room.

No telling what she saw, one teacher told me
nose frowned into showers
of red x's dripping from
her lips. My student tells me

what she sees now:
The current of her caregiver's
combustion; the clause
of her life just short

of predicate and period.
The mom she refuses
to adopt yells
she will have my job
because her daughter

cannot do shit like that.
I'm a good woman,
she tells me, *I am
a liar,* she roars

split tongue forking

poison into my ears,
a wound licker opening places
meant to heal. She does
not see her daughter's

scales, armor she grew
while her mother died
in front of her and inside of her;
she does not know this little girl

came into the world
fisting smoke inside her.
I crane her neck
to notice this black girl's light:

she knows how to read
herself—slow story stitched
with small stillness. She
loosens her quiet.

Look inside her, I say.
Her mother's shouting
begins. Her heart
contains you, you, you.

I hear this woman's shout
as cry. Sometimes,
ashes on the mouth
of my phone.

II.
Yesterday, D called and said
Do you remember Mr. _____?
All I could think was how
he made me laugh,
took the days' fodder
and spun it into glass
we used to look at ourselves.
Like when they found asbestos
In my room after several
years of complaints.
He coughed *It's a wonder*

We're not all dead! How
his weak tooth wiggled, how
I could see his cavities
all the time during laughs.
When the principal yelled
during meetings, Mr. _____
tucking tiny candies and typing.
I saved notes he wrote
during our principal's lectures:
Get me out of here.
Smile like you're afraid.
My offering: toothy smiles
trapped behind my hand.
D said he killed himself
yesterday. How was he
alone, this man who
offered us him, his
everyday sweetness
without expectation.
How he still blooms,
even here at the funeral
when all I hear
are stems pushing past
dirt, fighting to surface
the first petal and our
students' laughs glisten
off this page and my
knocks still scavenge
for candy or, please,
name this poem
and I will call you love.

· 2 ·

HONORING HOMEPLACE: CENTERING YOUTH AND COMMUNITY SCHOLARS AS CO-CONSTRUCTORS OF CURRICULUM AND RESEARCH

Miranda Goosby, Valentina Gamboa-Turner, and Erica R. Dávila

> "Pain is important: how we evade it, how we succumb to it, how we deal with it, how we transcend it"
> —Lorde in Winter, 2004, p. 16.

In the summer 2020, we (the authors) engaged with high school scholars in Chicago in naming and developing primary sources documenting their own truth in navigating the COVID-19 global pandemic and the disruption of normative forms of schooling. Building on the work of Audre Lorde, the scholars and community scholars (educators/teachers) evaded, succumbed, dealt with and transcended our collective pain as we engaged one another's life stories. This chapter is an attempt to share our story with the aim to engage educators and scholars to consider how ideological frameworks that center Black women can help us make meaning and as Lorde reminds us, transcend pain.

The Sojourner Scholars program was founded by Audrey Petty (www.audreypetty.com) and sponsored by the Illinois Humanities:

> Sojourner Scholars provides high school students from four South Side Chicago Public high schools the opportunity to take college level courses with local university and college faculty over the course of three summers. In the final summer, students embark upon a research-intensive capstone project that draws upon local, community-based archives and resources. (Illinois Humanities, 2021)

While this program consists of multiple cohorts every summer with a specific curriculum; this chapter will focus specifically on the work with a cohort of high school seniors in summer 2020 in a research-intensive capstone project that occurred as the culminating portion of the program. The curriculum consisted of research protocols, we worked together to investigate the ways in which research has been co-opted from communities of color and how we can rewrite our own narratives as research to be analyzed by us and for us. To support these inquiries, the authors and the scholars engaged in a multitude of theoretical frameworks and methodological protocols including autoethnography, Black Feminist Theory, Chicana epistemologies and Critical Race Theory (CRT). CRT informs the research questions we ask, the methodologies we employ, and the ways we analyze data. Solórzano and Yosso (2002) offer five elements to consider when engaging critical race theory and methodology in education; "The intercentricity of race and racism with other forms of subordination; The challenge to dominant ideology; The commitment to social justice; The centrality of experiential knowledge; and the transdisciplinary perspective" (pp. 25–27). We considered all five of these elements in analyzing the artifacts from our teaching experience with the Sojourner Scholars in the summer of 2020. However, the element that anchored this article is the centrality of experiential knowledge. "[This element] exposes deficit-informed research and methods that silence and distort the experiences of people of color" (Solórzano & Yosso, 2002).

We engaged with multimedia text, participated in peer-to-peer knowledge construction and dialogue with community elders, scholars, and healers. Together, we created a space where we critiqued the lack of Black/African-centered curriculum and pedagogy in their traditional school experience in Chicago, and this shared experience as students and alumna (two authors attended the same school district as the scholars)connected us, we reflected back to our own experience in Chicago in the 1990s and the current lived experiences of these youth in the same district 30 years later; still struggling with normative theories (and practices) of education that consistently leave students and families of color at the margins. As the community scholars that cultivated this program, we honor the parallels of Sojourner Truth's freedom-fighting and the legacy of movement building for educational equity in Chicago.

Following this introduction, Goosby (first author) offers an introspective counternarrative in an autoethnographic entry. Next, we offer a brief discussion of our planning process as the three authors played a key role in the process of co-constructing the curriculum. Finally, we offer a closing discussion offering our conditions for collective praxis anchored in hooks' (1990) homeplace.

An Autoethnographic Reflection: *We were reflections of one another*

The first author (Goosby) served as Program Coordinator/Teaching Assistant within Sojourner Scholars summer program in 2020. Goosby served as a generational bridge between the two instructors (Gamboa-Turner and Dávila) and the high school scholars. We recognize the challenges but most importantly the necessity of intergenerational intellectual work. It is critical for movement-building and justice-centered work to co-create learning spaces and by default classrooms. Therefore, we value the intergenerational space that the summer program offered as well as the journey of crafting this manuscript. Below, Goosby offers an autoethnographic reflection that we share here as part of our data. The authors chose to have this portion as a standalone piece of data because of the power of Goosby's introspection in her own words:

> I am influenced by Sojourner Truth's words "the truth is powerful and will prevail" in my academic life. I surround myself in worlds and spaces that care about the person as a whole, in all aspects. I've worked with the program for the past year and it's honestly been one of the most inspiring experiences in my career. Entering the last two weeks of Sojourner Scholars Summer Institute 2020 from July 13–July 24, 2020 allowed me to harness a deeper understanding of our capstone students' feelings, dreams and realizations living life in now "COVID-19" 2020. Experiencing conversations like David Stovall's expansive, genuine and raw academic and personal perspective on the education system exposed me and the students to how connected all of Illinois specifically is and how the lack of access and educational disparities within marginalized communities is not an accident but more of a plan. Annissia Collins [one of the scholars] asked the class during our discussion with Stovall "if we feel that America funds white supremacy and police brutality" and in return the answer is yes. Breaking down how deeply embedded the racial, structural, and systemic oppression is within this country and within Chicago, allowed students to grow in a desire to combat the injustices but also know that they are not alone. In our last week, Ru'Gia Jones (a teaching assistant) and I interviewed each other about our roles within the program and the presence of intergenerational Black feminism in our lives. We discussed what feminism meant to us. We discussed how Black women's melanin is made of stardust, it is found within the stars. Working with her, opened my eyes to see what the Generation Z world is creating, how they are feeling, and how brilliant they are. I myself learned a lot from her as she is an entrepreneur at 19 years old and believed in her work enough to follow her dreams despite what others may have said.

Our conversations within my personal conversation with Ru'Gia Jones were also inspired by talks the collective had with Anänka Shony, Ann Aviles, Asif Wilson, Timothy Mays, and Brence Turner. Their insight into what your career path can be, whether it includes pursuing a degree within higher education overtime or not at all, both inspired us to know that there are not any limits to our capabilities. Each student's work itself was an intimate and well-developed look into their lives. As a collective, we were reflections of one another. Sojourner Scholars Summer Institute 2020 was a portal. A portal to where I learned that the instructors and the students were interchangeable roles, both guiding and growing the group, creating new ways of thinking, expressing, and owning the power in one's words and presence. Gamboa-Turner and Dàvila and I entered the space with an open mind, allowing the space to share its gifts with us in its own time with guidelines but not with immediate expectations.

Goosby's reflection embodies hooks' framing of homeplace as a site of resistance and liberation struggle; she shares the ways in which the practices and approaches cultivated a homeplace for her and the scholars. She also highlighted the power of having the intergenerational insights shared regarding career and life expectations that are rooted in liberation and self-determination ... as the community experts of color all reminded the scholars of their power to determine their own futures. The dialogue that Goosby shared with Ru'Gia exemplifies the power of the co-constructing knowledge and decentering the norms of teacher/student role which crystallizes the ways the scholars challenged dominant ideology, and centered experiential knowledge.

Co-creators of Curriculum and Co-constructing Knowledge

> I want to speak about the importance of homeplace in the midst of oppression and domination, of homeplace as a site of resistance and liberation struggle. (hooks, 1990, p. 385)

One of the most enriching moments in this collective pedagogical experience was the co-construction of knowledge in the curriculum development as Goosby described above as a portal of sorts. Early in the summer of 2020, when no one knew the impact of the COVID-19 global pandemic or the racial uprising following the murder of George Floyd; the three authors came together to co-construct this research-intensive capstone project for high school seniors, all of whom identified as Black or mixed race (Black and Latinx). While many more people were involved with the curriculum planning, including Audrey Petty (program founder) and Ru'Gia Jones (teaching assistant). The three authors (Goosby, Gamboa-Turner and Dávila) worked closely together on the curriculum development before the youth scholars started the course as well as during the duration of the program, meeting often between daily class sessions. This co-creation and co-construction of curriculum is not common, especially for high school curricula.

We worked together to create a framing of the course while leaving room for the scholars to give their input with everything from establishing community in an online course, choosing content like music and resources connected to their stories. Leveraging our work as critical education scholars, we centered practices that centered the youth scholars. During our time planning the course curriculum we came together to share all of our experiences doing research, both informally and formally, to really brainstorm the purpose of the research project and how to best support the scholars. As the scholars engaged with public intellectuals and community activists in Chicago, we were able to develop research tools, conduct and transcribe interviews and most importantly lead the analysis and meaning making of the data. Our theoretical frameworks of Black Feminism and CRT guided our teaching/learning as well as the analysis of our experience working with the youth. We lean on research methods that affirm our theoretical standpoints. Through the development of curriculum within this framework we were able to stretch past the limitations of centering—whiteness or using only the (master's tools) to understand the way we research and seek to document.

As deeply rooted Chicago scholars we offer an intergenerational framework around solidarity and social justice legacies of Chicago's educational movements as a starting point for our summer capstone program. Also embedded in our praxis is an understanding that as Latinas (authors 2 and 3) utilizing Black Feminist framing we take on the full weight and responsibility of honoring the legacy and labor of Black feminist theorists. We are aware of our positionality and the ways in which parts of our identities and lived realities in Chicago serve as a bridge for cultural proliferation with the Black scholars that we built within this program; however, we are also aware of the sacred moments and realities that are completely theirs and not for us. Anzaldúa (1990) names the "difference between appropriation and proliferation is that the first steals and harms: the second helps heal breaches of knowledge" (p. xxi). Within solidarity acts, positionality should remain in focus and met with great care. Our work as women of color scholars is to work within these frameworks of solidarity and embody authentic acts that build and repair the harm that institutionalized research methods often inflict on our communities.

The global pandemic of 2020 has added yet another layer of struggle in a city and school district (all the high school scholars in the program attended the same public school district) with a deep history of education void of Audre Lorde's vision and work. The summer experience shared in this chapter probed and leaned into Lorde's legacy and work to deconstruct systems of oppression that anchor many learning spaces for Black and Brown people in this nation.

Unearthing Y/Our Story and Homeplace

Through critical dialogue, the scholars, teaching team and community guests/speakers documented the repetitive structures of oppression and domination that have impacted Chicago public school students' experiences. Together, we explored the work of several Black Feminists, especially the work of bell hooks on homeplace. The scholars learned and illuminated their beloved histories, these counternarratives exemplified the joy and potential of learning spaces that are justice centered; instead of the traditional learning spaces that constantly push children to the margins or worse. We revisited the program materials, including syllabus, student, and instructor notes, and most importantly the work that the youth scholars generated.

Given the state of the world in summer of 2020 with many unknowns and uncertainty the scholars engaged in the framing of homeplace. As hooks (1990) offers:

> We could not learn to love or respect ourselves in the culture of white supremacy, on the outside; it was there on the inside, in that homeplace, most often created and kept by black women, that we had the opportunity to grow and develop, to nurture our spirits. (p. 384)

One of the scholars, Na'Kiya Nash-Prince, interviewed her mother and grandmother to learn more about Chicago's history and her grandmother shared how gentrification and disinvestment of certain communities was part of their family story stating, *We didn't lose the house, the state bought it because they wanted to build a crosstown highway.* As Petty (2013) found "For thousands, the outcomes have included displacement, multiple moves, and homelessness. In the current economy, the poverty rate is higher than ever in Chicago, as is the need for affordable housing" (p. 16). The outcomes discussed by Petty (founder of the Sojourner program) hit close for the scholars who shared their family stories of displacement and lived realities of unsecured housing. Building on Audre Lorde's (1987) theorizing the anger of Black women and racism situates Na'Kiya's narrative within a broader social context of racism; "Any discussion among women about racism must include the recognition and the use of anger. This discussion must be direct and creative because it is crucial" (para. 20). Lorde's work affirms the anger we endure as women of color navigating the consistent institutional racism that anchors urban removal in cities like Chicago.

As critical scholars, we understood how these actions are calculated and part of a larger urban removal agenda that leaves people of color from low-income communities at the margins. Although the community scholars did not realize the theme of homeplace would conjure discussions about urban removal in Chicago; hooks' framing offered the youth scholars as well as the community scholars a powerful perspective of the need for homeplace, especially given this history. The scholars understood the power of sharing and learning from our own narratives and how to work as a collective to resist these realities as generations before us have done to claim our spaces in our communities of Chicago. We argue the summer capstone course created a space where we leveraged our stories to push social change in our own spheres of influence, and equally important the scholars were able to affirm one another as they shared their family stories and were able to see the parallels of the institutional oppression as well as the power of their communities fighting the oppression.

The framing of homeplace took on a new meaning since our home was now a virtual classroom and the teachers and scholars met and connected fully over a video meeting platform. The community scholars took time to consider what it meant to build community or a homeplace online. Some of the ways we did this included leaning into hooks articulation of home, in which we are our whole selves at home, we belong. The scholars did a lot of reflection and introspection aiming to name the ways their homeplace saved them during the pandemic. Not just our program but their actual homes where many of us were quarantined and had new appreciations for our homeplace. "[Homeplace] was about the construction of a safe place where black people can affirm one another and by doing so heal many of the wounds inflicted by racist domination" (hooks, 1990, p. 384). By reclaiming our "homeplace" as a sight of healing and justice-centered learning we moved experiential intergenerational knowledge to forefront. Unapologetically centering our experiences and our elders' experiences in schooling. We held our collective experiences up to the light and developed art, poetry and research that reflected our truth. This was not an exercise in justifying or glorifying "damage-centered" (Tuck, 2009) analysis of schooling in Chicago rather a critical act of interrogating our experiences and developing something other than narratives that continually dehumanize our communities and families. Not only where we vested in breaking the deficit narratives about our schooling experiences, we also made efforts in transforming narratives that budded up during the beginning of the pandemic that put more emphasis on how COVID-19 disrupted normative capitalistic values of consumption and individualism and the possibilities of how being in our homes could be an opportunity to cultivate new ways of engaging ourselves our communities and learning. We all became hyper aware of the ways in which biological conditions such as the COVID-19 virus can lead to a restructuring of our everyday lives.

At the outset of our program. we collectively crafted our agreements or consejos:

> I agree to love/respect myself and others
> I agree to be accountable for what I do and say
> I agree to handle conflict with respect
> I agree that my gifts bring value to the space
> I receive the gifts that the space offers me.

These agreements or consejos, crafted anchored our program and served to honor and support the well-being of the scholars. These statements push up against the traditional learning spaces that are most focused on what NOT to do; instead, we name what we collectively agree to DO. These statements represent the cultivation needed for the scholars to craft their counternarratives or unearth their stories; and reflect critically on homeplace. We all looked inward to cultivate a learning space that centered us and our stories, also known as counternarratives in the field of CRT. Collectively, we shared all the ways we have been silenced and/or marginalized in school.

The Sojourner Scholars program aimed to shift this dynamic and instead of curriculum and policies not designed for the progress of people of color, we chose to unearth the stories of the high school scholars, our community elders and public intellectuals rooted in the work of educational equity in Chicago. Annissia Collin's, one of the high school scholars crafted a "I Remember" poem on unearthing herstory and part of that poem reads,

> I remember ... Another year ... Another breath Contemplating if accepting the past for what was and what wasn't will strengthen my optimism for a more peaceful

future ... The terror in the tale but looking ahead I shall never fail ... The blood sweat and tears to forgive will encourage my drive to love with no hesitation ... A fight so strong but a love so deep ... Reminds me of honeycomb colors that shined through my window as I slowly opened my eyes from long nights sleep.

Annissia's poem provides a vivid expression of struggle and hope, while not naming the specific struggles we can hear her unearthing herstory of resilience and resistance. Furthermore, Donita Verner and Ru'Gia Jones unearthed their family stories connected to the COVID pandemic in an interview dialogue.

Donita: my grandma, she has real bad asthma and she gets sick real quick ... we not going to go over ... I do not want to get it and go over there and now she got it and she has asthma and it's like fatal on people who have asthma and then my niece cannot go over there because she can give her a regular cold then it's easier for my grandma to catch corona. Ru'Gia: yeah my great grandmother she ain't been outside since February, she has not touched the front door since February ... so I understand completely.

The story of the COVID-19 pandemic must be told by the communities who endured the brunt of this public health crisis that we are still enduring today in the summer of 2022. This critical dialogue in the summer of 2020 in Chicago between our teaching assistant, Ru'Gia Jones and scholar Donita Verner (who is the 2021 teaching assistant) demonstrates the necessity of unearthing our stories.

One of the scholars shares an account on how she understood intergenerational feminism represented in her family without initially having the language for what she saw. While engaging with Black feminist literature, she shares that; "Black women create portals of freedom within their homeplace." This idea of portals of freedom builds on hook's (1990) framing of homeplace:

In our young minds houses belonged to women, were their special domain, not as property, but as places where all that truly mattered in life took place—the warmth and comfort of shelter, the feeding of our bodies, the nurturing of our souls. There we learned dignity, the integrity of being; there we learned to have faith. The folks who made this life possible, who were our primary guides and teachers, were black women. (p. 383)

An interview between Ru'Gia Jones and Jasmyn Petty exemplifies the impact of intergenerational Black women for them:

Ru'Gia: Do you feel that intergenerational Black feminism occurs within your household?

Jasmyn: *I have seen an example from my mom, my grandmother and myself... I am just like my mother, I take on a big role in my household.*

Ru'Gia: *I feel like that's in my household too, we are really pro-independent women... you should be able to stand on your own and be self-sufficient.*

As Lorde (2007) states, "For women, the need and desire to nurture each other is not pathological but redemptive and it is within that knowledge that our real power I rediscovered ... this real connection which is so feared by a patriarchal world" (p. 110). These counternarratives highlight how the youth and community scholars beautifully provided regarding their homeplace; both literal and metaphorical homeplace.

Next, we will close with a discussion that offers our ideas of intergenerational engagement on homeplace, healing-centered and transformative praxis that cultivates the conditions for justice-centered learning communities in Chicago. As critical scholars and women of color we aim to center the voice and power of our next generation and our ancestors.

Closing Discussion

This program ran in July of 2020 when we were all anxious, angry and yet invigorated between the global pandemic, coping with the collective trauma of the murder of George Floyd and the racial uprising. Given this context, in addition to the concept of homeplace, Lorde's (2007) framing of anger anchored our work in the summer of 2020. Almost everyone in the world was dealing with loss, be it loss of loved ones, loss of jobs, loss of celebrations, loss of public transportation, lack of food for many communities, etc. Our city was hit hard, especially the communities in which the scholars reside. Infused in all the anger was growth for a new generation that could change the world. As Lorde (2007) states, "the same way I have used learning to express anger for my growth" (para. 5). The youth scholars in Chicago were expressing their anger with a racist (in) justice system and having the opportunity to work with a group of scholars that fit the profile of the youth racial uprising in Chicago we thought deeply about how to provide space so these scholars can express their anger for their growth as Lorde offers. The scholars used their anger as inspiration and collectively shared how their stories can bring change to the power structures around them.

But anger expressed and translated into action in the service of our vision and our future is a liberating and strengthening act of clarification, for it is in the painful process of this translation that we identify who are our allies with whom we have grave differences, and who are our genuine enemies. Anger is loaded with information and energy. (Lorde, 1987, p. 1)

As illuminated from these counternarratives by Chicago scholars, we all had an opportunity to engage a learning community that mirrored hooks' "homeplace" and evoked Lorde's declaration, "the master's tools will never dismantle the master's house." Thus, crafting and cultivating our own tools that center intergenerational engagement on homeplace, healing-centered praxis that cultivates the conditions for justice-centered learning communities in Chicago. The scholars included methods of collective care that included discussions and events aimed at taking care of our mental and physical health at an unprecedented time in our nation, the peak of a global health pandemic coupled with the racial uprisings; the scholars were in the heart of the unfolding events in Chicago in the summer of 2020. Thus, the authors/scholars decided to craft an intentional space devoted to caring for ourselves and families/communities; we believe the narratives we share will add to the conversations for more justice-centered practices in Black and Brown urban communities.

The power of the collective is the space that can be held. Space to process the conditions that have so many of us struggling and unjustly pushed into the margins of humanity. The opportunity and the challenge of working in collective praxis is that certain conditions are critical to hold a safe and fertile building community; we name these three conditions as follows: (1) establishing consejos/agreements together with the whole learning community; (2) commitment to collective care including lifting as we climb; and (3) transparent communication rooted in love. We would like to close with quotes from the scholars' poetry that encompasses so much of our collective praxis and healing in the summer of 2020 in Chicago:

> "I remember the everyday feeling of wanting to do something as if to jump into how my best self would look like"—Cassandra Hickmon
>
> "I am from ... Stay together & be back before the street lights come on."—Armani Easter

References

Anzaldúa, G. (1990). *Making face, making soul. Haciendo caras: Creative and critical perspectives by feminists of color.* Aunt Lute Foundation Books.

hooks, b. (1990). *Homeplace. Yearning: Race, gender, and cultural politics.* South End Press.

Illinois Humanities. (2021). Sojourner Scholars. https://www.ilhumanities.org/program/sojourner-scholars/

Lorde, A. (2007). *Sister outsider: Essays & speeches by Audre Lorde.* Crossing Press.

Lorde, A. (1987). The uses of anger: Women responding to racism. *Women and Language, 11*(1), 4.

Petty, A. (2013). *High rise stories: Voices from Chicago public housing.* McSweeney's.

Solórzano, D. G., & Yosso, T. J. (2002). Critical race methodology: Counter-storytelling as an analytical framework for education research. *Qualitative Inquiry, 8*(1), 23–44.

Tuck, E. (2009). Suspending damage: A letter to communities. *Harvard Educational Review, 79*(3), 409–427.

Winter, N. (2004). Audre Lorde. In J. W. Hall (Ed.), *Conversations with Audre Lorde.* University Press Mississippi.

· 3 ·

ENGAGING A RADICAL POETICS OF HEALING BY DESIGN: ON POIESIS, DISOBEDIENCE, AND THE PURSUIT OF LIBERATED SELVES

Phillip A. Boda

Where to begin. Over the years I've tried to make sense of my own positionality in relation to those I've been charged to serve in education. This commitment has been driven with aims to help me develop concerted efforts in both focused and tangential ways that disrupt the status quo of our current free-market-driven educational system. What draws parallel across all my pursuits has been a commitment to making anew those contexts that have, for so long, embodied, and emboldened the normative center of schooling (Leonardo & Broderick, 2011). By this term—the normative center—I mean those affective, discursive, and material artifacts that, as Mikhail Bakhtin (2013) teaches us, subject those participants in, and consumers of, communal practices and dialectic praxes to define cultural mores as monolithic entities that invariably develop/sustain unquestioned strata of value in society.

This normative construction, then, leads to axiological commitments to methodology and epistemic-centering praxes that are embodied within and through the contours of our psyche as socio-linguistic ways of Knowing and Being in the world. As such, normative centers, and the historiographical impact this Hegemony produces, make our views permeable to (macro)narratives and define the Narration of Self, Other, and society via Personhood and identity. I also mean those material realities that scholars such as Enrique

Dussel (2013) and Walter Mignolo (2002, 2007, 2009) argue manifest as structural formulations of (his/her/their) stories *designed with specific purposes* to deny agency and power to those deemed most dispensable to Western Capitalistic Global (Imperial)isms.

Increasingly, one thing I know we must do in education to move toward more just futures for all, and specifically those multiply marginalized in society more broadly, is to (re)design for Healing from the wounds of past atrocities and oppressive structures. We must delve into the affective elements of teaching and learning if we are to create a more just future that affords all students the opportunity for *causal agency* (Shogren et al., 2017). In other words, "[people acting] with an eye toward causing an effect to accomplish a specific end or to cause or create change in his or her life … [toward] enhanced self-determination" (p. 17). In turn, in order to broach the subjective innate in the personal as a dialogic interplay between Self, Other, and society in ways that will disrupt formalized oppressive hegemonies, we must make things anew; we must disobey past methods of Being/Knowing.

In this pursuit of Self within and through a lens that will liberate all body-mind-spirits, our shared path is intimately tied to the Healing that must occur for those most subject to vulnerability: Those living at the nexus of multiple marginalization (Collins, 2019). In this chapter, I take up this charge by unpacking what poiesis and disobedience have to do with the pursuit of liberated Selves in educational contexts for various stakeholders within and across multiple levels. I then provide implications to this work to urge all of us as critical pedagogues toward futures not yet known and trouble myopic approaches to designed structural social justice without a concomitant, and interdependent, approach to pursue Healing as we reproach the injustice of this world. Through this work, I invoke a plurality of perspectives that serve to evoke multiple layers of affect, pushing toward a cognitive-systemic architecture of Liberation.

What Does It Mean "to Heal," to Move Toward a Place of Healing for Our Selves and Others

As we stave through the COVID-19 pandemic and work through the virulent rhetoric and propaganda that it has burgeoned around "Freedom" and "Rights," there is a need to address how and in what ways we can (re)approach our collective purposing of education. One crucial way to do this is through

Healing. Meaning, that we can no longer sit idle while the current educational industrial complex barrels toward solutions for some while keeping the status quo intact for all. In this way, I draw on bell hooks and her articulation of Healing and Love-as-Service to help us think with and through the crucial importance of the affective in relation to critical education:

> Love in action is always about service, what we do to enhance spiritual growth. A focus on individual reflection, contemplation, and therapeutic dialogue is vital to healing ... To truly serve, we must always empty the ego so that space can exist for us to recognize [i.e., witness; Oliver, 2001] the needs of others and be capable of fulfilling them. The greater our compassion the more aware we are of ways to extend ourselves to others that making healing possible. (2000a, pp. 216–217)

In this excerpt, bell hooks teaches the transformative potentialities of love as service to others. Throughout this text, hooks illuminates the power of cultivating our keen awareness to *interdependence*. Through fluency of each other's interdependence, hooks makes the case that while we often advocate to be wary of co-dependence, our notions of dependence need not fall prey to blanket exclusions. In other words, we almost never talk about how all human beings on Earth are interdependent—that we exist and thrive when we can articulate and manifest a world where we value the connections between each other. In education, interdependence shows up to support familiar affiliations, and/or sustain alienations, that emerge among each of our lived experiences of culture (Emdin, 2010), while also urging us to engage with liminalities within and among positional identities often set in juxtaposition rather than unpacked with a relational discourse of commonality (Shelton, 2020). By recognizing the importance of interdependence, then, we find a need to disrupt "what is" in favor of future (re)designs where those most vulnerable to violence are Healed and truly valued.

Wanda Watson (2018), further, encourages thought around the charge we have as teacher educators in relation to our collective stakeholder understandings of classroom spaces and student positionalities where sociocultural and epistemic injustice continue to thrive. She contends that "... teacher educators, teachers, and policy makers must take up politicized care in ways that help various stakeholders construct their awareness of a particular context and determine approaches that resonate with them within that context" (p. 375). Indeed, Watson revisits tried and true critical pedagogical lenses that help us disrupt attempts to depoliticize education under the guise of neoliberalism and in the face of evidence that learning environments are, never have been, and never will be, devoid of political textures (cf. Cooper & Gause, 2007; Giroux, 1988; McLaren & Farahmandpur, 2001). This argument speaks to the notion of Healing as an act of subversion, of radical awareness, and of Love wherein to Heal is to actively use one's individual, proxy, and collective agency (Bandura, 2018) to change the world in ways that improve the lives of all who live on this planet. Similarly, we must not forget about the importance of these agentic decisions as we know all too well that if left to its own devices, education as a form of socioeconomic stratification will persist (Cole, 2005).

Watson continues their charge for teacher educators by stating that our roles must engage new teachers to "... interrogate their own purposes for being educators; guiding them in ways that move them away from superficial ego-driven factors towards those rooted in a sense of interdependency" (2018, p. 375). Here, we see further emphasis placed on interdependence as a transformative component to understanding how classrooms are politicized with and through hegemonic assumptions unquestioned at multiple stakeholder levels, expounding on the importance of how we envision our Selves in relation to Others. In this way we emphasize the notion of healing as, first, a (re)cognition—a rethinking—about what is essential for the liberation of Self from structural designs that sustain educational injustice. Moreover, this witnessing of the important role interdependence plays in our creation of the world anew then supports us moving beyond what is expected in educational spaces where we have learned our "tricks of the trade," "disciplinary commitments to standards," and "classroom management strategies" to support new ways to envision possibilities of creation that have seemingly infinite potentialities. This process pushes us to encounter the act of *poiesis*, and the poetics of life innate in the fabric of all methods of Becoming and Being: Toward a Radical Poetics of Self.

Poiesis as the Enactment of a Radical Poetics of Self

In 1997 Édouard Glissant's seminal book *Poetics of Relation* was translated to English and in it his arguments shed light on gestures toward Being and Beingness that are integrated *in relation* to geo-historical and bio-political artifacts embodied in the affective, discursive, and material realities of life (see Mignolo, 2002). Glissant, drawing from Deleuze and Guattari, contends: "Rhizomatic thought is the principle behind what I call the Poetics of Relation, in which each and every identity is extended through a relationship with the Other" (p. 11). In this way, Glissant is arguing through an anti-colonial discourse challenging subjugation to present an idea of Becoming and Being, of *poiesis*, as always a relational quality and subjectivity: That there can be no centering without the concomitant creation and sustainment of the marginalized as dispensable via "deficit ways of Being" and "unsophisticated ways of knowing."

hooks (2000b) and Collins (2019) also teach us this lesson through more pragmatic implications of this rhetoric in relation to how identity emerges in the context we learn and are exposed. Collins denotes challenges to these specific colonial designs through Liberation theory and coins them "resistant knowledge projects" (2019). Through this articulation, Collins argues for an ever-evolving poiesis—of *critical praxis*: "Critical social theories cannot be defined solely by what they opposed in the past, they also have to make the case for what they are for, and why that matters now" (2019, p. 89). In sum, both Glissant and Collins ground a need for radically reimagining life, and the education of life, as relational praxes that demand responsive shifts to not embody a centralization that denies agency, subjectivity, and Personhood.

These works also push us to think beyond binary assumptions we hold about how the world "is" and encourage us to move toward what we seek it "to Become": What acts of poiesis are necessary to engage the unpacking of social positionings imperative to anti-colonial projects toward dismantling all hierarchies of power (Collins, 2019; Mignolo, 2009)? In education, these types of structural and intersectional analyses have led to the development of approaches to disrupt the normative center from which those historically marginalized are often measured and deemed deficient. These include, but are not limited to, critically analyzing within-group assumptions made about student peers that require de-settling to highlight ways to support resilience among multiply marginalized youth in disciplinary spaces (Leyva, 2021), that reading-researching gender across levels challenge hegemonic interpretations of identity used to deny students agency to self-determine (Kean, 2020), and challenging the historiographical pretense of myopic definitions of "quality" in relation to how we educate all students to read themselves and the world (Souto-Manning & Rabadi-Raol, 2018). All of which work anew contexts that have previously been designed to assimilate in ways that both change such designs and, in turn, Heal.

These calls align with a sense of re-making Self and Other, as well as the contexts that sustain their oppositional constitution as a requirement for understanding one's place and value in the world. To challenge these contexts, thus, requires that we, first, identify and describe the textures of these sites of historical multiple marginalities based on geo-historical and bio-political artifacts. Then, these critical scholars call upon us to change these contexts *by design*: To engage with the act of Becoming and Being as a dialectic critical praxis whereby Self and Other both enmesh their positional identities in these contexts in ways that embody the process of (re)creation, affording students the opportunity for a re-consensus of Rights (i.e., Calabrese-Barton & Tan, 2020). This requires an approach to education that explicitly disrupts the status quo beyond changing practice and/or interaction: It demands that we fundamentally shift the ways in which we construct our understandings and envision their value. This critical call, thus, requires us to disobey the epistemic center we draw, while supporting Others to do so as well.

Disobedience as a Necessity for Justice

The expansion of Western capitalism implied the expansion of Western epistemology in

> all its ramifications, from the instrumental reason that went along with capitalism and the industrial revolution, to the theories of the state, to the criticism of both capitalism and the state ... It is no longer possible, or at least it is not unproblematic, to "think" from the canon of Western philosophy, even when part of the canon is critical of modernity. To do so means to reproduce the blind epistemic ethnocentrism that makes difficult, if not impossible, any political philosophy of inclusion ... [emphasizing that] colonial difference is reproduced in its invisibility. (Mignolo, 2002, pp. 59, 66, 73)

Here, I am drawing from among broader philosophies of Liberation and world-systems analytics that have challenged the centralization of Becoming and Being through "rooted" epistemic frames (i.e., Glissant, 1997). These realities manifest in our individual and among our collective ideological state apparatuses used to develop our senses of Self, Other, and society (Althusser, 2014). My contribution to this argument unpacks the coloniality wedded in designs we create and sustain among educational contexts and subjects used to help students frame their understandings. These arguments about the onset of Modernity and the coloniality of power that were developed as part of the broader capitalist project of transnational globalization fit nicely into an understanding of the world and its institutions as having specific purposes that were *by design*. For example, schooling emboldens the meso-narration of positional identity that some students are inherently "smarter" than others (Hatt & Urrieta, 2020; Sengupta-Irving, 2021) and that students' performative embodiments are representative of deficit cultural affiliations (Gholson & Martin, 2019; Wright, 2019). Further, by-and-large, scholars of social justice in education have neglected more peripheral identities such as disability in attempts to disrupt the normative center, thereby sustaining either/or analyses (see Pugach et al., 2021). What, then, is needed to challenge these assumptions that manifest epistemic injustice? I argue this is uniquely aligned with the above philosophers to de-link these centerings entirely: To disobey *episteme*.

In his 2012 book, *Local histories/Global designs*, Mignolo contends that our traditionally embodied epistemic commitments (our formally consecrated *episteme*) are not the opposite of less formalized personal opinion and common shared beliefs (*doxa*). Instead, they provide an alternative approach to this juxtaposition that can de-link from the coloniality of power wedded in and furthered through the boundaries sustained by this dichotomous categorization of value related to who can be producers of knowledge, and whose knowledge is there to be consumed through the project of modernity: *Epistemic Disobedience*. Mignolo suggests that the status quo which we regard as the acceptable collection of knowledge leveraged by people in sociocultural learning contexts (our methodologies) and the ways in which we treat subaltern formulations and descriptions of lived realities (our epistemic commitments), are designed to value a (white/able) Western Modern construction of colonial subordination.

When given power and authority to define truth about Self and Other, this approach positions and pits mono-categorizations of difference against each other to embody "divide and conquer" strategies. In turn, an approach to socially just research embodying *epistemic disobedience* demands we problematize our inquiries of difference to disrupt hierarchies in research that can, when not viewed critically, position overlapping and marginalized axes of difference as constituting lesser "Othering" praxes deemed lower on hierarchal positionings of need (e.g., Pugach et al.'s 2021 critique of intersectional analyses *sans* disability). Such inquiries of difference deny the importance of identifying discrimination in context as the basis of intersectionality (Collins, 2019), further sustaining the geo-historical and bio-political coloniality that positions white, able-bodied, English-speaking, Christian, straight men as the center.

The argument I am making here about dismantlement of oppressive designs through "resistant knowledge projects" (Collins, 2019) and subsequent Healing needed from these former structural commitments that subjugate those outside the normative center, is to disobey these former colonial cartographies drawn up to create and sustain social hierarchies. This means that this process of creating the world anew—imagining classrooms beyond that which we were exposed—is a process of critical praxis, through which develops a sense of Becoming and Being that can radically change the course of peoples' lives for the better. In this way, the path toward a disobedient *episteme* being embodied by stakeholders in education, and then designed in contexts to embolden the liberation of Self from binary epistemic centering, is subject to an interplay between "what is" and "what could be": These praxes are part of a loving poetics that may wax and wane but ultimately charge teachers to continually Become, as June Jordan teaches us, "the ones we are waiting for"—to engage with an act of Poiesis-as-Healing.

This need not be merely theorized as an implementation process but, rather, that those engaging with this poetic process are subsequently also Healed by their critical social theorizing in ways that (re)make their Selves new and more aware of the cultural affiliations and alienations that subject those most vulnerable to violence daily in schools. This formative critical praxis of disobedience and the radical poetic Being that emerges from such a poiesis process reclaims the "Other" beyond marginality to embody what Patricia Hill Collins argues is the ultimate path for intersectionality as a commitment to "an open-ended process of creative social action, incorporating the ideas and actions" of various knowledge projects to not further sustain the normative center of society that is designed to bound, maim, and kill (2019, p. 188). It is with the framing on the importance of poiesis, disobedience, and the pursuit of liberated Selves that we can suggest applications for Healing and develop activist Healing as part of our praxes.

Embodying and Emboldening Designs to Heal: Epistemic and Positional Justice for All

Speaking about the future of the Feminist Revolution in the United States that developed throughout the multiple waves of Feminisms in the 20th century, bell hooks (2000b) reminds us that, like Angela Davis 15 years later (2016), *Freedom is a constant struggle*: "Our emphasis must be on cultural transformation: destroying dualism, eradicating systems of domination. Our struggle will be gradual and protracted" (p. 165). Both Radical Black Feminist scholars urge a view of the world without, but not forgetting the power and positioning practices designed into "historical precedence," as we have yet to see and experience a sociality and cultural emergence of Self, Other, and state where those multiply marginalized are free from violence and subjugation when defined and measured *in relation to* the cis-gendered, white, male, able-bodied, heterosexist normative center of society. Dorinda Carter-Andrews and her team of Black Female scholars in their 2019 study confirms that such injustice persists in many aspects of Self and Other for young Black girls in today's schools and schooling praxes:

> These girls were beholden to the impossibility of conforming to and embodying White cultural norms ... The White supremacist and patriarchal logics that undergird U.S. sociopolitical life were evident and operating ... in ways that dehumanized Black girls' bodies and limited the enactment of Black girl authentic identities. (p. 2564)

They go on to frame what is required for multiply marginalized youth such as Black girls in schooling contexts specific to the role teachers play in this process around agency and identity:

> Educator pedagogy and practice should also draw from varied disciplinary theories and frameworks for developing instruction and school policy that affirms and integrates Black girls' whole selves into the learning experience. As long as Black girls contend with society's perpetuation of perfection and femininity as an embodiment of whiteness, schools will not be a place where they can practice epistemic or identity agency, and simply *be* while learning. (Carter-Andrews et al., 2019, pp. 2564–2565, emphasis in original)

In sum, this work on Black Female education scholarship draws explicitly from Black Feminist Thought, Liberation theory, and world-systems analytics more broadly in the sense that:

1. The struggle for any Liberation of Selves from hegemonic systems positioning some students and Personhoods as less-than by virtue of their identity is, and will continue to be, an ongoing critical praxis of (re)forming our Self and our relationship with Others;
2. Such a radical poetics of transformation of Self and Other through poiesis demands that we disobey the systems and practices that sustain this unjust hegemony by design; and
3. Within and among our attempts to engage with poiesis as a praxis of relationality through our disobedience of epistemic centering that creates whiteness as the normative center, we must Heal our past wounds to not have them trickle onto those we seek to serve.

These authors and the philosophers expounded above recognize the importance of Self in relation to internalized oppression and argue that it can be leveraged to develop Healing praxes for our Selves, Others, and society to shift from oppositional to relational praxes (Keating, 2012).

Coming back to the need of educators to understand their Selves in relation to Others (i.e., the coloniality of power wedded in institutions), the need to actively fight against the grain of current educational praxes that devalue the personal in pursuit of the depolitical, and the violence systems enact *by design*, Patricia Hill Collins teaches us the importance of agency and self-determination across Being/Becoming, Knowledge/Knowing, and Healing-Transformation: "Epistemic oppression relies on specific strategies that reproduce social inequality ... [and] suppresses the epistemic agency of some members of the group while elevating that of others, thus producing privileged and derogated categories of knowers" (2017, pp. 118, 120).

In other words, Collins (2017, 2019) reading Carter-Andrews et al. (2019) and Watson (2018) would advocate for an in-depth excavation of our personal Selves—both those we perform in specific contexts and those we leverage for authority (Mensah & Jackson, 2018)—that would lead to a change in the way we think about making decisions in relation to interpretations of the actions of Others. This approach invariably leads to a shifting from a reliance on the ways of Knowing and Being that our Selves are familiar with, which we often pit in opposition to those we are less familiar with (Emdin, 2010; Shelton, 2020), toward the development of an *episteme* and *doxa*—our formal and informal bodies of knowledge from which we draw when enacting individual, proxy, and collective agency (Bandura, 2018)—that no longer seeks to juxtapose white Western knowledge systems, and the power invested in those identities, against positionalities and ways of Knowing outside of that *normalized epistemic centering of value*.

To develop Epistemic and Positional justice for all, I argue, demands we engage with this radical poiesis of *epistemic disobedience* where the central purpose of our work is to Heal *by design*. This is not a small ask for teachers, administrators, and researchers in education. Indeed, as I have shown above, even those engaged in social justice teacher education have relinquished a wholistic intersectional approach to analyzing the unjust treatment of students based on the education designs embodied in the schooling process when talking about race, class, and gender at the exclusion of disability (Pugach et al., 2021), which I and colleagues have challenged via the status quo of our educational endeavors (cf. Boda, 2021; Kulkarni, 2021).

This should not, however, deter our commitments to make the world anew through a more critical view of the word and the world; rather, it should invigorate us to think with and through previous analyses done in social justice education circles in ways that support our colleagues and those they are charged to serve multiply marginalized students with the means to engage with the radical Poetics of Becoming—of *poiesis*. This type of work engages all educational stakeholders, again, to recognize the importance of interdependence in relation to understandings of Self, Other, and society, and do so such that the designs that have drawn up histories of exclusion in education are disobeyed, with their epistemic centers dismantled.

Working toward these liberated futures of Self, then, requires we begin with a goal to Heal—our Selves and Others—and subsequently start the path toward Healing as one such crux to support that a democratic embodiment of humanity is part and parcel to the ways we extend our individual agency to support radical collective change for the (re)creation of this world as a Home for all body-minds-spirits (Berne et al., 2018; Kulkarni et al., 2021; Michalko, 2009).

This task holds less impact if we also do not specifically design our schools to support all Souls to embrace Love, be Loved, and Love Others. This, then, follows a Radical Intersectional Ethics of Care many scholars have devoted their lives toward the disruption of the normative center across multiple disciplines in order to help multiply marginalized students see value in their Selves, as well as employs us to unpack ways of Knowing, Being, and Feeling connected to cultural affiliations and various communal praxes that disobey the normative centering of schools where Love and Healing is not just invisible but denied (cf. Cariaga, 2019; Hall, 2021; Nicol & Yee, 2017; Raghuram, 2021). Emphasizing this radical poetics in the context of schools, and following through with such a caring, Loving, Healing critical praxis echoes the late Gloria Anzaldúa in a final essay she wrote, *Let us be the healing of the wound*:

> We must bear witness to what our bodies remember, what el corazón con razón experiences, and share these with others ... These healing narratives serve not just self-nurturing "therapy," but actually change reality. We revise reality by altering our consensual agreements about what is real, about what is just and fair. We can transshape reality by changing our perspectives and perceptions. By choosing a different future we bring it into being ... May we do the work that matters. Vale la pena. (2005, pp. 313, 314)

References

Althusser, L. (2014). *On the reproduction of capitalism: Ideology and ideological state apparatuses*. Verso Trade.

Anzaldúa, G. (2005). Let us be the healing of the wound: The Coyolxauhqui imperative—la sombra y el suefio. In A. Keating (Ed.), *The Gloria Anzaldùa reader* (pp. 303–314). Duke University Press.

Bakhtin, M. (2013). *Problems of Dostoevsky's poetics* (Vol. 8). University of Minnesota Press.

Bandura, A. (2018). Toward a psychology of human agency: Pathways and reflections. *Perspectives on Psychological Science, 13*(2), 130–136.

Berne, P., Morales, A. L., Langstaff, D., & Invalid, S. (2018). Ten principles of disability justice. *WSQ: Women's Studies Quarterly, 46*(1), 227–230.

Boda, P. A. (2021). The conceptual and disciplinary segregation of disability: A phenomenography of science education graduate student learning. *Research in Science Education, 51*, 1725–1758.

Calabrese Barton, A., & Tan, E. (2020). Beyond equity as inclusion: A framework of "rightful presence" for guiding justice-oriented studies in teaching and learning. *Educational Researcher, 49*(6), 433–440.

Cariaga, S. (2019). Towards self-recovery: Cultivating love with young women of color through pedagogies of bodymindspirit. *The Urban Review, 51*(1), 101–122.

Carter Andrews, D. J., Brown, T., Castro, E., & Id-Deen, E. (2019). The impossibility of being "perfect and white": Black girls' racialized and gendered schooling experiences. *American Educational Research Journal, 56*(6), 2531–2572.

Cole, M. (2005). Cross-cultural and historical perspectives on the developmental consequences of education. *Human development, 48*(4), 195–216.

Collins, P. H. (2017). Intersectionality and epistemic injustice. In J. Kidd, J. Medina, & G. Pohlhaus (Eds.), *The Routledge handbook of epistemic injustice* (pp. 115–124). Routledge.

Collins, P. H. (2019). *Intersectionality as critical social theory*. Duke University

Cooper, C. W., & Gause, C. P. (2007). "Who's Afraid of the Big Bad Wolf?" Facing identity politics and resistance when teaching for social justice. *Counterpoints, 305*, 197–216.

Davis, A. Y. (2016). *Freedom is a constant struggle: Ferguson, Palestine, and the foundations of a movement*. Haymarket Books.

Dussel, E. (2013). *Ethics of liberation*. Duke University Press.

Emdin, C. (2010). Affiliation and alienation: Hip-hop, rap, and urban science education. *Journal of Curriculum Studies, 42*(1), 1–25.

Gholson, M. L., & Martin, D. B. (2019). Blackgirl face: Racialized and gendered performativity in mathematical contexts. *ZDM, 51*(3), 391–404.

Giroux, H. A. (1988). *Teachers as intellectuals: Toward a critical pedagogy of learning*. Greenwood Publishing Group.

Glissant, É. (1997). *Poetics of relation*. University of Michigan Press.

Hall, A. R. (2021). Towards love as life praxis: A Black queer and feminist pedagogical orientation. *Communication Teacher, 35*(3), 262–275.

Hatt, B., & Urrieta, L. (2020). Contesting the Alamo and smartness: Theorizing student identities, agency, and learning within the contentious practices of US classrooms. *Theory Into Practice, 59*(2), 202–212.

hooks, b. (2000a). *All about love: New visions.* HarperCollins.

hooks, b. (2000b). *Feminist theory: From margin to center.* Pluto Press.

Kean, E. (2020). Advancing a critical trans framework for education. *Curriculum Inquiry, 51*(2), 261–286.

Keating, A. (2012). *Transformation now!: Toward a post-oppositional politics of change.* University of Illinois Press.

Kulkarni, S., Nusbaum, E., & Boda, P. (2021). DisCrit at the margins of teacher education: Informing curriculum, visibilization, and disciplinary integration. *Race Ethnicity and Education, 24*(5), 654–670.

Leonardo, Z., & Broderick, A. (2011). Smartness as property: A critical exploration of intersections between whiteness and disability studies. *Teachers College Record, 113*(10), 2206–2232.

Leyva, L. A. (2021). Black women's counter-stories of resilience and within-group tensions in the white, patriarchal space of mathematics education. *Journal for Research in Mathematics Education, 52*(2), 117–151.

McLaren, P., & Farahmandpur, R. (2001). Teaching against globalization and the new imperialism: Toward a revolutionary pedagogy. *Journal of Teacher Education, 52*(2), 136–150.

Mensah, F., & Jackson, I. (2018). Whiteness as property in science teacher education. *Teachers College Record, 120*(1), 1–38.

Michalko, R. (2009). The excessive appearance of disability. *International Journal of Qualitative Studies in Education, 22*(1), 65–74.

Mignolo, W. D. (2002). The geopolitics of knowledge and the colonial difference. *South Atlantic Quarterly, 101*(1), 57–96.

Mignolo, W. D. (2007). Delinking: The rhetoric of modernity, the logic of coloniality and the grammar of de-coloniality. *Cultural studies, 21*(2–3), 449–514.

Mignolo, W. D. (2009). Epistemic disobedience, independent thought and decolonial freedom. *Theory, Culture & Society, 26*(7–8), 159–181.

Nicol, D. J., & Yee, J. A. (2017). "Reclaiming our time": Women of color faculty and radical self-care in the academy. *Feminist Teacher, 27*(2–3), 133–156.

Oliver, K. (2001). *Witnessing: Beyond recognition.* University of Minnesota Press.

Pugach, M. C., Matewos, A. M., & Gomez-Najarro, J. (2021). Disability and the meaning of social justice in teacher education research: A precarious guest at the table?. *Journal of Teacher Education, 72*(2), 237–250.

Raghuram, P. (2021). Race and feminist care ethics: Intersectionality as method. In *The Changing Ethos of Human Rights.* Edward Elgar Publishing.

Sengupta-Irving, T. (2021). Positioning and Positioned Apart: Mathematics Learning as Becoming Undesirable. *Anthropology & Education Quarterly, 52*(4).

Shelton, S. Z. (2020). Integrating crip theory and disability justice into feminist anti-violence education. *Canadian Journal of Disability Studies, 9*(5), 441–463.

Shogren, K. A., Little, T. D., & Wehmeyer, M. L. (2017). Human agentic theories and the development of self-determination. In *Development of self-determination through the life-course* (pp. 17–26). Springer.

Souto-Manning, M., & Rabadi-Raol, A. (2018). (Re)centering quality in early childhood education: Toward intersectional justice for minoritized children. *Review of Research in Education, 42*(1), 203–225.

Watson, W. (2018). We got soul: Exploring contemporary Black women educators' praxis of politicized care. *Equity & Excellence in Education, 51*(3–4), 362–377.

Wright, C. G. (2019). Constructing a collaborative critique-learning environment for exploring science through improvisational performance. *Urban Education, 54*(9), 1319–1348.

· 4 ·

BECOMING LBS: EXPLORING AMBITIONS AND TENSIONS IN (DE)CONSTRUCTING A HUMANIZING UNDERGRADUATE TEACHER PREPARATION PROGRAM

Laurie Inman and Jen Stacy

As faculty in undergraduate teacher preparation at a Hispanic Serving Institution, we believe that the process of *becoming* more fully human is one of unfinishedness: we are incomplete beings with unfinished realities who have awareness of our incompleteness (Friere, 1972, p. 84). In conjunction with developing critical consciousness about unjust social realities, this awareness motivates us to take action against oppressive forces while continuously engaging in generative and dialogic education—a progressive strive for liberation. Carter-Andrews et al. (2019) identifies participation in sustained critical self-reflection as one key factor to a humanizing approach to teacher education. As faculty, we understand our critical reflection to be a layered dialogue that builds among each other, our classroom experiences with pre-service teachers, and the realities of PreK-12 schooling. The following co-generative dialogue tells our department's unfinished project of humanization in which we continuously puzzle through how to dismantle teacher preparation and build it anew in the image of justice.

Laurie: In our Liberal Studies Department (LBS), we are immersed in marginalized BIPOC communities, therefore our focus on justice and equity seeks to personalize our students' experience. It is critical that we facilitate students' development so they become critically conscious educators who acknowledge and

	engage in difficult conversations and reimagine equitable and responsive learning environments in which they will teach.
Jen:	Absolutely. Redesigning our program happens through everyday dialogue, albeit during hallway conversations, syllabus revisions, or even a complete overhaul of programmatic components. We understand our program development to be a type of generative praxis—our "reflection and action upon the world in order to transform it" (Freire, 1972, p. 51). While we try to guide students in forming praxis, we are constantly developing our individual and collective critical consciousness as we grapple with theory, program/course design, practices, and infrastructural realities.
Laurie:	I think you would agree that this is not always easy in a growing department as our diverse perspectives around justice and teacher preparation are illuminated. There is the natural collision between our identities, scholarship, and lived experiences, yet we do share common theoretical frameworks that guide the work and provide a solid foundation for the changes that we recognize must be made to improve early preparation. In our collective efforts toward critical consciousness (del Carmen Salazar, 2013), we have identified the need for significant changes in our program and curriculum.
Jen:	Absolutely! This has resulted in ongoing conversations that require us to slow down, listen deeply, and ask pertinent questions that, quite honestly, sometimes seem like they derail us. Questions emerge around the reliance on some scholars over others, teaching frameworks, assessment tools (are rubrics really the best tool if they replicate unquestioned standardization?), and even the extent to which teacher education should reflect the teaching practices of our local districts. These rabbit trails make the work less linear and messier but also requires us to really see each other.
Laurie:	Speaking of our local districts ... A key part of teacher preparation is the clinical experience and talk about messy. We have great partners, yet our students are constantly telling us that what they are learning is not seen in their host classrooms. For example, our Responsive Teaching and Learning class is focused on culturally responsive and sustaining pedagogies, trauma informed practices, and other key concepts around learning. Candidates are exploring what it means to engage children in active purposeful ways that focus on funds of knowledge (Moll et al., 1992), community cultural wealth (Yosso, 2005) and are student-centered. Unfortunately, what they observe is often in direct conflict to their learning as too many educators are perpetuating colonist ideologies and deficit mindsets in classrooms where our students are placed. Changing the infrastructural realities of placement is definitely a challenge.
Jen:	Centering critique in clinical practice is necessary but adds so many layers of difficulty. Another challenge is navigating neoliberal structures as we (re)imagine our program. Innovation is often met with technocratic demands that dehumanize teacher education.

For example, we recently revised our critical multicultural education class to meet the university's graduation writing requirement, opening an opportunity to push back against typical institutionalized writing.

Laurie: Much conversation was had about which content should be privileged (foundational theories or contemporary scholars?) and what exactly liberatory writing in education entails.

Jen: I saw this as a chance to upend the traditional essay that suppresses ethnically and linguistically diverse students' voices while others stated that access to this format is essential for mainstream success beyond our program, because at some point they will be asked to write that traditional research paper. While we know from Audre Lorde (1984) that "the master's tools will never dismantle the master's house," what do we owe our undergraduates whose teaching career will demand post-baccalaureate success?

Laurie: I believe the answer to that question lies in our intentional interrogation of our program and the decisions we make to affirm and validate the cultural and linguistic resources of our students. When I think about the early discussions about changing our Introduction to Teaching course, we agreed the traditional almost canonical prototype that teaches from a missionary-save the children perspective needed to go. The next iteration was not clear to everyone, and it seemed the discussion halted. Now it is designed to explore how Native/Indigenous Peoples, the African Diaspora, Asian Americans, Latinx, working-class Whites, Abled, Queer, and Gendered Lives have experienced education within the framework of power and privilege and what we can do as future educators to transform and empower communities of learners. What an evolution!

Jen: And I suppose sometimes we recognize that not always agreeing is central to our unfinished becoming. Our dialoguing is a form of teaching and learning amongst ourselves—as we teach, we learn and as we learn, we teach (Freire, 1996). I love sharing successes that represent these dialogic layers of both faculty and student becoming, like the student who created a podcast using Spanish, Mixe, Zapotec, and English and featured her grandfather talking about language learning, culture, and immigrating from Oaxaca to Los Angeles.

Laurie: That is a clear example of one tenet for humanizing teacher education pedagogy defined as "enacting ontological and epistemological plurality" (Carter-Andrews et al., 2019, p. 21). The fact that there are numerous ways of knowing and being with multiple modes and media that can be used for expression in assignments; and the resources that we use are expansive and highlight scholars of color. We affirm future teachers' humanity and facilitate strengths-based and reflective mindsets.

Jen: Equally valuable are our reflections of what is not working. Much of this involves deconditioning years of schooling and internalized oppression, which sometimes prevents us from articulating new possibilities. Grades are an example of symbolic violence; yet they are expected by both students and the institution.

	I once tried abolishing grades and my students revolted—they did not feel like this was a humanizing approach, despite my explanation, and what I thought to be loving praxis!
Laurie:	Discussing these conundrums becomes co-generative curricula: permitting us to see systems of power in operation, pushing us toward more just practices. Each time we think we have advanced; we recognize that we have only increased our awareness of our own unfinishedness.

This glimpse of praxis through dialogue showcases our efforts to humanize undergraduate teacher preparation. Making our process visible demonstrates how we operationalize critical theories at the programmatic, curricular, and interpersonal levels (Carter-Andrews et al., 2019) and how this process is never finished—it is reflective of and generated through our becoming.

References

Carter-Andrews, D. J., Brown, T., Castillo, B. M., Jackson, D., & Vellanki, V. (2019). Beyond damage centered teacher education: Humanizing pedagogy for teacher educators and preservice teachers. *Teachers College Record: The Voice of Scholarship in Education, 121*(6), 1–28. https://doi.org/10.1177/016146811912100605

del Carmen Salazar, M. (2013). A humanizing pedagogy. *Review of Research in Education, 37*(1), 121–148. https://doi.org/10.3102/0091732x12464032

Freire, P. (1972). *Pedagogy of the oppressed*. Penguin Education.

Freire, P. (1996). *Pedagogy of freedom: Ethics, democracy, and civic courage*. Rowman and Littlefield Publishers.

Lorde, A. (1984). *Sister outsider: Essays and speeches*. Crossing Press.

Moll, L. C., Amanti, C., Neff, D., & Gonzalez, N. (1992). Funds of knowledge for teaching: Using a qualitative approach to connect homes and classrooms. *Theory Into Practice, 31*(2), 132–141. https://doi.org/10.1080/00405849209543534

Yosso, T. J. (2005). Whose culture has capital? A critical race theory discussion of Community Cultural Wealth. *Race Ethnicity and Education, 8*(1), 69–91. https://doi.org/10.1080/1361332052000341006

· 5 ·

BELONGING DESPITE BORDERS: AN AUTOETHNOGRAPHIC RESPONSE TO U.S. IMPERIALISM, MIGRATION, AND IDENTITY

Van Anh Tran and M. Yianella Blanco

Prologue

Belonging is often conceived as feeling a part of an existing social, economic, or political order (Castles, 1998; Sidhu, 2018). Migration interrupts such notions of belonging due to the ways power embedded within institutions form new patterns of migration and settlement. Though typically framed as a "choice," migration is often forced upon individuals and families due to systemic issues that make their lives in their home countries untenable—either due to violence, poverty or, increasingly, climate-related disasters perpetuated by policies enacted by neo-imperialist interests. In other cases, families are violently uprooted and displaced due to war, left dispossessed and without the ability to return to their homelands.

Many of these causes are inextricably linked to capitalist and white supremacist power structures which render the lives of those in the "global south" as expendable. U.S. interventionists practices, like those of Europe and other imperial powers, began as a "racist economic project that constructed much of the Global South as places whose lands and people must serve white capitalist interests" (Abrego & Villalpando, 2021, p. 63). While U.S. media, popular culture and school curricula often frame migration as one that is a choice, or that migration to the United States is the desired outcome by most migrants themselves, the reality is that the decision to leave one's home is often deeply painful. Even when families believe that their only option for survival is to migrate, the process of coming to such a decision is agonizing. Troubling our understanding of how, when and who migrates shifts adds to our perspective about the interconnectedness of empire and migration. Central America and Southeast Asia serve as two regional examples that experienced and continue to experience the devastating effects of U.S. intervention. By centering both, it becomes evident how the United States expanded its capitalist economy and attempted to secure its position as a global superpower during the mid to late 20th century. Further, centering the stories of migrants from Central America and Southeast Asia (and the descendants of this generation) provide an axis of analysis for the tension between the United States's demand for racialized labor and to disseminate its ideals and the nativist, anti-immigrant demands that economic and political opportunities be reserved for those conceived as authentic "Americans." Tangibly, it influences the extent to which immigrants, and children of immigrants, experience belonging in their new communities.

For educators, not only is understanding these varied connections between migration, empire, and power essential curricularly, but it also presents the multidirectional nature of belonging in their own classrooms. Learning is relational and that a sense of belonging is required within the community, school, and classroom level. The effects of migration are not theoretical, but rather felt and experienced in classrooms all around the country.

Yianella

I grew up with Central America in my home, but never in my studies. As a child of the Central American diaspora, I remember beginning every school year by receiving my new social studies textbooks and skimming through the pages, eagerly searching for at least one mention of Costa Rica or Nicaragua. I searched for one, small acknowledgment of our contributions or simply, our existence. I searched for validation for me, my family, and others like us; I looked for reasons that explained my family's movement, their sacrifices, and their joy. In my 12 years of primary and secondary education, Costa Rica was never mentioned once, at least not in the textbooks. I usually found Nicaragua in our books at least once, but always and only in relation to the Iran-Contra scandal. I did not have the political language or education then to understand what prompted me to do this every year or to describe how these silences, at best, and the perpetuation of military violence stereotypes, at worst, affected the way I understood myself, my family, and my own history. It was not until college and graduate school that I began to truly learn the histories of Central America, including our resistance movements, that were not defined or written by Americans.

While grateful to finally have access to this knowledge, it caused me to wonder why *my* history was an elective, accessible only through higher education, while the history of white Americans and Europeans were considered the standard curriculum. Armed with this question and the memories of searching for myself unsuccessfully in school, I carried myself through my teacher preparation program and now, graduate school. As an instructor in my graduate program, I proposed and developed a course focused exclusively on Central American history for pre-service teachers. The aim was to introduce our students to this history so that it may disrupt their understanding of the region, the current immigration/border "crisis" and to provide tools so that they may pass it down to their future students as well. The aim was for Central American students to not experience the same silences that I did.

Still, despite knowing the importance of including our histories and experiences, the process of developing and facilitating the course led to several existential crises that I grappled with throughout the two semesters I taught the course. As I sat down to create the syllabus, I found myself stunned into inaction: *Am I the right person to teach this? What do I really have to say, teach, pass on? What if I get things "wrong" or don't "authentically" capture, tell or teach the experiences of Central America(ns)? What is "authentic" anyway and who gets to decide?* The pressures and fears of whether I was knowledgeable *enough* or "authentically" Central American *enough* brought me back to when I was a student flipping through textbooks searching for faces like mine. Here, I wasn't questioning where I fit within American history narratives, but whether I fit within Central American ones.

Empire, Imperialism, and Migration

As global axes of power shifted throughout the 19th century, the United States attempted to secure its position within such hierarchies. The United States implemented its expansionist ideologies by engaging in "103 interventions in the affairs of other countries between 1798 and 1895" (Zinn, 2000, p. 2). Then, emerging from World War II as a "superpower," along with the Soviet Union, ideological and material conflicts between capitalism and communism during the subsequent Cold War saw these nations expand their spheres of influence to different regions of the world (Zinn, 2000). U.S. imperialism and empire were "born out of a process of colonialist expansionism and [for which] white supremacist racism provided an ideological basis" (Gaido, 2016, p. 72). These ideological differences served as a convincing cover for the United States' insatiable desire for more power and, thus, intervention and exploitation of many countries around the world.

Central America

Though Central Americans have been migrating to the United States throughout the 20th century, U.S.-backed civil wars in El Salvador, Guatemala, and Nicaragua fueled large numbers of migration throughout the 1980s and 1990s (Garcia, 2006; Gzesh, 2006). Since then, "peace-time" Central America has had to contend with the fallout from such civil wars; natural disasters, including the most recent, devastating hurricanes Iota and Eta (Ishizawa & Miranda, 2019); the mass deportation of Central Americans, who had joined gangs that were created in U.S. cities (Arana, 2005; Lovato, 2020); climate change-induced droughts (Aguirre, 2020; Harvey et.al., 2018); and drug wars (Martinez, 2013, 2016). Then, in 2009, the United States again supported a right-wing coup against the democratically elected President Manual Zalaya in Honduras, which has had devastating effects in the country (Frank, 2018). All of these conditions have led to and continue to contribute to the displacement and forced migration of thousands of Central Americans all along the isthmus.

Southeast Asia

In different contexts, Southeast Asia (SEA) may include countries such as the Philippines, Thailand, and more. For the purposes of this chapter, however, Southeast Asia is a political and social organizing identity that encompasses those having roots from the countries of Cambodia, Laos, and Vietnam. This identity uplifts those who experienced war and genocide in the mid to late 20th century, causing a mass exodus into resettlement countries, such as the United States. While grouped together in this way, it is crucial to recognize the heterogeneity of these communities based on culture, educational experience, ethnicity, language, socioeconomic status, and more. The experiences of SEA refugees are entwined with "complex histories of colonialism, imperialism, and war" between the late 19th century and the end of the 20th century (Vang, 2016, p. 88). The U.S. government was heavily involved in Cambodia, Laos, and Vietnam to combat the spread of communism. Occupation during the Khmer Rouge genocide in Cambodia, bombings in Laos, and war in Vietnam claimed millions of lives between 1955 and 1975 (SEARAC, 2020). Following the occupation, war, and genocide, there was a mass migration of SEA refugees from the region.

Van Anh

Named after two celebrated women warriors who led the Vietnamese peoples' first major revolts against colonialism, the Hai Bà Trưng School for Organizing launched in the summer of 2011. At the outset of the weekend-long retreat, facilitators and participants engaged in a collective dedication activity reflecting the Vietnamese spiritual history of honoring those who have come before. During this opening activity, everyone in the space approaches the altar, one by one, to leave a picture or memento of the person to whom they want to dedicate the training. While participants can talk about who the person is and why they are dedicating the training to them, there is no requirement to speak. This beginning segment is not the only opportunity that participants have to share their stories; throughout the weekend, there were cycles of reflective, community-building, educational, and action-oriented activities and workshops offered moments for participants to pause, engage, reflect, and commune.

I would have dedicated the training to my dad.

My dad was one of five—the oldest son. A few years after he was born, he and his family migrated to the South after Vietnam was partitioned by decision-makers in a city nearly half a world away. His mother passed on when he was 14, and a few years after that, he was conscripted to the South Vietnamese navy to be part of a war effort that seemed to be going on for as long as he could remember.

The stories of not only Vietnamese refugees, but also those in the greater Southeast Asian diaspora who fled the region after the social, political, economic, and military turmoil during and after the war in Vietnam—including Cambodian, Hmong, and Lao refugees—live within the communities themselves, contemporary art and literature, and emerging academic research studies. But it was community-based, grassroots efforts, such as the Hai Bà Trưng School, which first held space for me to remember, reconstruct, and reflect upon these stories. It was within organizing spaces that I was politicized—where I learned to draw connections between my family's stories and those across various diasporic communities, where I began to understand the ways in which our liberation is tied to one another. Before I had the language to express how I felt, I knew that my ways of knowing and being were deeply entwined with my history, the history of my people, and the power that sits within our minds and spirits, as our bodies have been displaced. Thus, the choices that I have made to enter the teaching profession and, later, to return to graduate school have been grounded in a belief of the necessarily interconnectedness of our stories, memories, and identities. It is with this in mind that I hoped to engage with community-based programs as a part of my scholarship.

Partnering with communities, however, raises ethical and reflexive considerations that pushed me to rethink whether I should even be doing this work. Community spaces taught me to name power dynamics, after all. As I was developing my pilot study proposal, I hesitated to initiate a conversation with community organizations about a potential research partnership. I did not want to "extract" stories and experiences from my communities. I was steeped in negotiating my identities as "researcher," "community member," and more. The pilot study proposal remained unfinished as I constantly asked myself: *Why am I doing this? Who am I accountable to?*

The Power of Narratives

The use of "narrative" has grown in popularity and has come to be interpreted in different ways across a variety of disciplines, but it is fundamentally understood to be related to the act of "storytelling" (Reissman & Quinney, 2005; Reissman & Speedy, 2007; Reissman, 2008). One of the reasons narrative has increased in popularity is because we experience stories everywhere, all of the time. As Barthes notes:

> Narrative is present in myth, legend, fable, tale, novella, epic, history, tragedy, drama, comedy, mime, painting... stained glass windows, cinema, comics, news items, conversation. Moreover, under this almost infinite diversity of forms, narrative is present in every age, in every place, in every society; it begins with the very history of mankind (sic)... nor has there been a people without narrative... it is simply there, like life itself. (as cited in Sontag, 1982, pp. 250–251)

Groups and individuals have used narratives to serve a variety of purposes—to remember, argue, justify, persuade, engage, entertain and even to mislead (Reissman, 2008). They have also been powerful tools for political change, to mobilize others, foster a sense of belonging and community. Stories themselves are "connected to the flow of power in the wider world (Reissman, 2008, p. 16)." They reveal important truths about human experience and the sociopolitical structures in which they exist.

Storytelling is what grounded our work for this book chapter. Its power as an emancipatory and healing tool, in addition to the cultural roots narratives have in our own respective heritages, assisted us in sharing and identifying the ways in which our lives, and those of our families, have been affected by migration and displacement caused by imperial violence. The use of narrative captured the depths of these experiences with each other.

Learning from Each Other

In reflecting on our upbringing as children of a displaced generation—the child of Costa Rican immigrants and the child of Vietnamese refugees—we began to see important similarities that spoke to the diasporic experience. Though the circumstances of our families' displacement vary widely, there was a richness in looking at these experiences, ones not often discussed, together. From there, our project was born. We drew from autoethnographic research traditions to draw out and engage with the rich, embodied knowledges that were passed down through us. Autoethnography, in particular, can produce meaningful and accessible research grounded in personal experience to underscore "experiences shrouded in silence" (Ellis et al., 2011) and "[illuminate] more universal patterns" (Lawrence-Lightfoot, 2005, p. 12). We opted to share our stories through letters that contained family photographs and short descriptive narratives of them. For us, family photos have always occupied a combined space of fragmentation, longing, and imagination. Neither of us have too many photographs from our childhood or of our respective families' pre-migration since the losing of those items are common due to displacement. Displacement causes not only material losses, "but also conceptual and nostalgic: the notions of home and of spaces of belonging are reconstituted as sites of memory" (Murrani, 2020, p. 174). For that reason, the photographs we do have are cherished as some of the few tangible connections we have to people and countries we used to call Home. Given the emotional weight of photographs, we knew they would generate important stories, anecdotes, and memories about who we are and how we came to be because of migration.

In addition to selecting photographs to share, we also wrote short descriptive narratives about each of them. To prepare us for these narratives, we developed specific probing questions. For example, we asked ourselves: "Who/what is in this photo?" "What emotions come up for me when looking at the photo?" "Why did I select this one?" "What would I want someone to know about this photograph?" We knew that revisiting these photographs would be an emotional task and so, borrowing from our pedagogical knowledge as teachers, we set up these scaffolded questions to help us process the photos, identify their significance to us, as well as how to communicate those thoughts with others.

Upon receiving and reading each letter, we added to a reflection journal, where we recorded elements of the letter that resonated with or raised questions for us. After sending, reading, and reflecting on each letter, we met to discuss them and recorded those conversations. We repeated this cycle a total of three times. We transcribed each meeting, letter, and reflection journal entry and then open coded them, seeking recurring themes, dissonances, and questions.

What emerged from this process was a transformational shift in how we understood our own knowledge and power. We each entered this process insecure about the authenticity or legitimacy of our own cultural knowledge due to our family's displacement. By laying bare these internal uncertainties—the questions, reservations, and hesitations—we quickly realized how they manifested themselves in our approach to teaching and research by diminishing the knowledge we already carry and bring. Going through this process elucidated how our memories, the stories passed down through us and our meaning-making of them, are already examples of knowledge, even if they are not always accepted as such. We have emerged from the project recognizing we are already armed with the necessary tools for dreaming and building toward collective free futures for our communities.

Our Questions and Uncertainties

Yianella: *In what ways do we feel authentically connected enough to our past, to our memories? Do we feel entitled enough to share them?*

Van Anh: *People have agency with their storytelling, and I wonder... I'm telling the story, like my story, but my story is not only my story... it's intertwined with all of these other people's stories, and one can't disentangle all of that.*

As educators and scholars whose work is intimately connected to our identities and experiences, we have often felt paralyzed by questions of our own authenticity as tellers and sharers of our stories. These hesitancies and insecurities have manifested not only in our private reflections, but also in the ways that we have made decisions about our public-facing scholarship. We often questioned our positionalities and considered the ways that we were complicit in decontextualizing our families' and communities' experiences. Yianella's quote reveals some of the internal questions raised in the initial phase of this project, such as "Am I remembering this correctly?" "How has my family remembered this incident? How similar or different is it from my own recollection?" The displacement of our families, and thus feeling like we are neither "fully" American nor "fully" Costa Rican or Vietnamese, resulted in constant questioning of whether or not we are in a position to remember, understand, or represent our histories well enough, much less in ways that does the richness and complexities of our communities justice. These internal struggles represent the insidious and continuous effects of displacement on our understanding of our identities. Displacement and migration strip us of the tangible pieces of our home, which results in the continuous questioning of our ability to claim our ancestral roots. While Yianella's quote reveals the internal questions we have grappled with, Van Anh's quote provides insight into how they affect our relationships and work within our communities as well.

As we move through our storytelling, we understand that the uncertainties and tensions that we feel are deeply connected to our commitments to and relationships with our families and communities. When we shared with one another, we often asked questions of ourselves; we regularly grappled with our memories and the ways that such memories and stories do not only belong to us (Dillard, 2006; Smith, 1999). Together, we traced the ways that our concerns were entwined with the legacies of displacement in our respective families and with the ways that we wanted to ensure that such legacies were honored and seen in all of their complexities. In questioning our own authenticity, we see the ways that we have internalized, not only external demands for justifying our histories, existence, and legitimacy (within and beyond our work as educators and scholars), but also the responsibility that we feel toward our people. We interrogate this notion of authenticity by understanding that our lived experiences encourage us to discursively produce and reproduce our ongoing understandings alongside one another. And so, we know that placing our memories in conversation allows us to map the ways that our individual stories and histories are also threads within a fabric formed through struggles for autonomy within systems of power. Even more so, we can see the overarching and the everyday acts and moments of resistance, survival, pain, and joy within ourselves and our families.

Building on what scholars of memory have elucidated about the relationship between collective memory construction (Halbwachs, 1992), social understandings of representations (Sturken, 1997; Landsberg, 2004), and witnessing (Murphy, 2019), we see that our combined meaning making of not only our family histories, but what they might mean in relation to one another, produces an affective, collectiveness consciousness that recenters us as actors within our memories. It is through our dialogue, then, that we are able to both hold ourselves and each other accountable *and* begin to shift how we conceive knowledge production. Understanding ourselves as actors within our family histories and seeing the responsibility that we feel to our families and communities as an asset, we are able to deeply consider our hopes for future generations and the ways that such hopes have been and will be enacted.

Our Dreaming and Building

Past, present, and future merged, mixed, and flowed in our conversations—we began to understand the ongoing and temporally fluid nature of our sensemaking. Situating ourselves in our present, as teacher educators and scholars, we identified tensions that we grapple with as we take into account our communities' histories, our families' histories, our histories. For Yianella in the design of her course on Central American History, she often wrestled with the realization that, for many of her students, this might be the first or one of the few interactions they have had with learning Central American history. The weight of presenting this history in ways that justly represented the full richness of the region impacted her curricular and pedagogical decisions. For Van Anh, at the outset of her research design, she knew that she wanted to work with the communities that held her throughout her life. And yet, she struggled to approach community organizations that she wanted to partner with because she understood the epistemic violence that institutions have committed against Black and Indigenous communities and communities of color (Smith, 1999). Our dialogue about the tensions that we experienced reinforced the way that diasporic reflections and understandings transcend fixedness. Rather, our continual self-questioning and self-doubts surfaced the "contingency, temporality, and displacement in space and time" (Murrani, 2020, p. 174) that we felt as we moved between uncertainty and a deep desire to disrupt dominant narratives and recenter not only our families' experiences, but also our own.

Recognizing that the construction of collective memories is an interaction between agents, cultural tools, and modalities (Halbwachs, 1992; Wertsch, 2002), we understand that our pedagogy is both informed by our stories and facilitates them. Tintiangco-Cubales (2014) defines pedagogy as:

> A philosophy of education informed by positionalities, ideologies, and standpoints (of both teacher and learner). It takes into account the critical relationships between the purpose of education, the context of education, the content of what is being taught, and the methods of how it is taught. It also includes (the identity of) who is taught, who is teaching, the relationship to each other, and their relationship to structure and power. (as cited in Tintiangco-Cubales et al., 2010, p. viii)

With this definition of pedagogy in mind, our dialogue pushed us to consider classroom practice and scholarship that not only centers the inclusion of narratives (content) in a thoughtful and nuanced way (methods), but also considers our identities, the identities of our students and those with whom we work, and the values and commitments that drive us (context and purpose).

Embracing our humanity and the humanity of our communities, we looked to our family histories as a way to understand ourselves in relation to those around us and to deeply reflect on how we have been informed by the interactions between our histories, our experiences, and our (dis)connections within contexts of migration. Our conversations showed us that there is both rootedness and movement in our experiences. In the same way that we are unable to disentangle the voices and experiences within our narratives and memories, we invite educators to disrupt linear and one-directional conceptions of time and power within storytelling. Leslie Marmon Silko (1981) expands our notion of temporalities and describes the relationship between storyteller and listener:

> The storytelling always includes the audience, the listeners. In fact, a great deal of the story is believed to be inside the listener; the storyteller's role is to draw the story out of the listeners. The storytelling continues from generation to generation. (p. 80)

In this way, our stories were drawn out of one another's stories. Yianella and Van Anh came to better understand our own family histories as we listened and engaged with the other's stories. We believe that educators can facilitate this process. In the classroom and within our scholarship, we understand that the way we claim our identities and the responsibilities that we have to our communities (Dillard, 2006) shifts the way that we see knowledge—where it lives, who produces it, how it is shared. For that reason, we are better able to facilitate and participate in storytelling that both humanizes those within the learning community and frames our/their stories and experiences as assets within the learning space that will support us all in being able to better understand ourselves and one another.

We start from a place of abundance and of care. While we have mourned the losses of people, places, and all that we will never know as a result of imperialism and displacement, we also realize that this critical reflection activates connections that we may have known but may not have always named. Being in community with one another and placing our stories in conversation—from a place of trust, love, and care—we expose the structures and relationships that cause us to question the brilliance and power that courses through our communities and ourselves.

What We're Holding

Nearly a year since beginning this project, we are sitting together with a newfound appreciation for not only the photographs our families have kept, but the stories, wisdom, and memories within them. As we sit within the past and future, we consider how we might begin this process all over again, but with new questions and prompts to further our understanding of ourselves and build stronger connections with our communities. With this new round, we might invite our family members to view and discuss the photos with us, to learn how they view them and what memories and feelings are raised for them in the process, as well as rebuild memories together. We may also extend some of our original questions by asking "Who are we responsible to? Who are these stories and memories for?" We may dig further within the wells of previous knowledge production to ask "Where do I know this knowledge from? Who did I learn it from and how?" "What from this do I wish to pass down to the next generation?"

As two women of color, educators, scholar-activists, daughters of immigrants and refugees, and so much more, we understand that our experiences, reflections, and considerations are informed by our intersectional lenses and positionalities. While we reflect on this process and how our identities impact our understandings of ourselves and our memories, we draw from Chicana/Latina feminist epistemological practices which remind us we must "confront aspects of ourselves that render us the colonized or the perpetrator (Calderón et al., 2012, p. 518)," particularly if we are working with marginalized communities, even if we are from those same communities. Though our reflections within this chapter consider the ways in which our identities have influenced our understandings of ourselves and our families, we are still cognizant of our privileges and are holding space for those who have not been given the opportunities we have to still remember, to still have at least some photos and family histories from which to draw upon and reflect. To hold space for those who, because of unjust systems of power grounded in white supremacy, sexism, homophobia, and ableism, continue to rob us of our homelands, our languages, traditions, and our memories.

As we consider how we will continue to move, we know that there is a deep love for our people that we want to bring forward with us. This love stems from our families' and communities' experiences, but also moves through and between our bodies. We think of the next generation, and we recognize the ways that they will build on our ways of knowing and being. For future generations of Central American and Southeast Asian young people:

We look into the future, and we see families, communities, and schools coming together, the boundaries that may be constructed between each in a different reality do not exist. Why would they? We have been, we are, and we will be informing one another, building together.

We look into the future, and we feel supported, seen, and loved. We have been, we are, and we will be embraced.

We look into the future, and we smell freshness, the mixtures of nature and our creations. We have been, we are, and we will be breathed.

We look into the future, and we taste old recipes and new. Shared foods that each can reach and enjoy. We have been, we are, and we will be savored.

We look into the future, and we hear the languages of our ancestors—the cadences, the beats, the remixes, and the shifts. We have been, we are, and we will be harmonized.

References

Abrego, L. J., & Villalpando, A. (2021). Racialization of central americans in the United States. Precarity and belonging: Labor, migration, and noncitizenship, 51–66.

Aguirre, J. C. (2020). In Central America, climate change is driving families North. Retrieved November 08, 2020, from https://www.sierraclub.org/sierra/2020-5-september-october/feature/in-central-america-guatemala-climate-change-driving-Families-north-climate-migration

Arana, A. (2005). How the street gangs took Central America. *Foreign Affairs*, 84(3), 98–110. https://doi.org/10.2307/20034353

Calderón, D., Bernal, D. D., Velez, V. N., Huber, L. P., & Malagon, M. (2012). A Chicana feminist epistemology revisited: Cultivating ideas a generation later. *Harvard Educational Review*, 82(4), 513–539.

Castles, S. (1998). Globalization and migration: Some pressing contradictions. *International Social Science Journal*, 50(156), 179–186.

Dillard, C. B. (2006). *On spiritual strivings: Transforming an African American woman's academic life*. State University of New York Press.

Ellis, C., Adams, T. E., & Bochner, A. P. (2011). Autoethnography: an overview. *Historical social research/Historische sozialforschung*, 273–290.

Frank, D. (2018). *The long Honduran night: Resistance, terror, and the United States in the aftermath of the coup*. Haymarket Books.

Gaido, D. (2016). *The formative period of American capitalism: A materialist interpretation*. Routledge.

García, M. C. (2006). *Seeking refuge: Central American migration to Mexico, the United States, and Canada*. University of California Press.

Gzesh, S. (2006). Central Americans and Asylum Policy in the Reagan Era. Retrieved November 08, 2020, from https://www.migrationpolicy.org/article/central-americans-and-asylum-policy-reagan-era

Halbwachs, M. (1992). *On collective memory* (L. Coser, Trans.). University of Chicago.

Harvey, C. A., Saborio-Rodríguez, M., Martinez-Rodríguez, M. R., Viguera, B., Chain-Guadarrama, A., Vignola, R., & Alpizar, F. (2018). Climate change impacts and adaptation among smallholder farmers in Central America. *Agriculture & Food Security*, 7, 57. https://doi.org/10.1186/s40066-018-0209-x

Ishizawa, O. A., & Miranda, J. J. (2019). Weathering storms: Understanding the impact of natural disasters in Central America. *Environmental and Resource Economics*, 73, 181–211. https://doi.org/10.1007/s10640-018-0256-6

Landsberg, A. (2004). *Prosthetic memory: The transformation of American remembrance in the age of mass culture*. Columbia University Press.

Lawrence-Lightfoot, S. (2005). Reflections on portraiture: A dialogue between art and science. *Qualitative inquiry*, 11(1), 3–15.

Lovato, R. (2020). *Unforgetting: A memoir of family, migration, gangs, and revolution in the Americas*. Harper, an imprint of HarperCollins.

Murphy, K. M. (2019). *Mapping memory: Visuality, affect, and embodied politics in the Americas*. Fordham University Press.

Murrani, S. (2020). Contingency and plasticity: The dialectical re-construction of the concept of home in forced displacement. *Culture & Psychology*, 26(2), 173–186.

Reissman, C. K. (2008). *Narrative methods for the human sciences*. Sage.

Reissman, C. K., & Quinney, L. (2005). Narrative in social work: A critical review. *Qualitative Social Work*, 4, 383–404.

Reissman, C. K., & Speedy, J. (2007). Narrative inquiry in social work, counseling and psychotherapy: A critical review. In J. Clandinin (Ed.), *Handbook of narrative research methodologies* (pp. 426–456). Sage.
Southeast Asian Resource Action Center (SEARAC). (2020). *Southeast Asian American Journeys: A National Snapshot of our Communities*. https://www.searac.org/wp-content/uploads/2020/02/SEARAC_NationalSnapshot_PrinterFriendly.pdf
Sidhu, R. (2018). A post-colonial autoethnography of transnational adoption. *British Journal of Social Work, 48*, 2176–2194.
Silko, L. M. (1981). Language and literature from a Pueblo Indian perspective. In L. A. Fielder (Ed.), *English literature: Opening up the canon* (pp. 54–72). English Institute.
Smith, L. T. (1999). *Decolonizing methodologies: Research and indigenous peoples*. Zed Books.
Sontag, S. (Ed.). (1982). *A Barthes reader*. Jonathan Cape.
Sturken, M. (1997). *Tangled memories: The Vietnam War, the AIDS epidemic, and the politics of remembering*. University of California Press.
Tintiangco-Cubales, A., Kiang, P. N., & Museus, S. D. (2010). Praxis and power in the intersections of education. *AAPI Nexus, 8*(1), v–xvii.
Tintiangco-Cubales, A., Kohli, R., Sacramento, J., Henning, N., Agarwal-Rangnath, R., & Sleeter, C. (2014). Toward an ethnic studies pedagogy: Implications for K-12 schools from the research. *The Urban Review, 47*.
Vang, C. Y. (2016). Southeast Asian Americans. In D. K. Yoo & E. Azuma (Eds.), *The Oxford handbook of Asian American history* (pp. 88–103). Oxford University Press.
Wertsch, J. V. (2002). *Voices of collective remembering*. Cambridge University Press.
Zinn, H. (2000). *The twentieth century, a people's history*. Harper Books.

· 6 ·

FRACTIONAL CRYSTALLIZATION AS A METAPHOR FOR A PALIMPSEST OF COLONIZATION

Meghan Zarnetske

We must unsettle our settler colonial beliefs in land as property. Whiteness and property are intimately entwined in American society founded on racial caste (Harris, 1993). The tenet of whiteness as property suggests that one not only has access to land but that land also contributes to one's power. In order to disrupt this, the assumption of power inherent in whiteness would have to be separated from land ownership. Calderon et al. (2021, p. 2) suggest "a disinvestment in Western epistemology as the single mode of knowledge, valuing non-Western expertise, and a shift from nature as external to being in relation to." Land is not a possession but rather a teacher, a part of our souls.

In scientific fieldwork, many disciplines rely on the land surface to gather data. In particular, geologists study both the surface and subsurface of the earth's crustal plates. This could be to find and extract natural resources, examine for earthquake potential, or measure the availability of water within a groundwater reservoir. All of these endeavors result in a capitalistic gain in conjunction with increased knowledge of geologic processes. For example, if a geologic team discovers a large reservoir of natural gas underground, they will then sell that information to a company intent on extracting said reservoir. The result of this extraction can be a polluted water reservoir for local residents, land subsidence, and damage to the land surface such that the local ecology is altered. Certain methods of extraction and geologic processes can be used as a metaphor for settler colonialism.

The geologic rock cycle of erosion, deposition, compression, and uplift is a continual process. So, too, is the work of settler colonialism. Settler colonialism describes the removal and erasure of Indigenous peoples in order for settlers to take over the land for their own use henceforward (Wolfe, 2006; Tuck & Yang, 2012). This colonization involves genocidal events as well as stealing land through treaties, and through congressional, presidential, and judicial acts. The Supremacy Clause in the United States Constitution is quite ironically considered the "Law of the Land." Often, treaties actually appropriate land through malicious wording and abuse of judicial power. Additionally, Indigenous erasure plays out in educational settings in that schools do not teach at all about the native peoples of North America, or what they do teach is essentialized or incorrect (Tuck et al., 2014). The only time Indigenous peoples are mentioned in mainstream media outlets are during times of crisis such as the #NoDAPL protests at Standing Rock and the current #landback movement for Indigenous lands and sovereignty to be acknowledged.

This paper is conceptual in nature. I begin by examining previous works by anti-colonial authors, specifically through the lens of how settler colonialism is an ongoing process that continually erodes the sovereignty of Indigenous peoples in the United States. I then weave in the geologic process of fractional crystallization as a metaphor, as well as examine current processes of settler colonialism and social movements for evidence of past movements, violence, and land/human conquest. Finally, I use this metaphor to apply a different lens to how settler colonial constructs of land could be reworked so as to take a more Indigenous perspective.

Acknowledging Time, Space, and Intention

In 2003, I was halfway through a Master's degree in geology. My intention then was to graduate and then find a profitable job in the oil and gas industry that allowed me to work outside. This goal was embedded in the narrative of white, capitalistic intentions that I mention here because I feel it important to state my positionality. As I interrogate settler-colonialism through a geologic metaphor, I speak of it as an extension of myself and not something I can fully extract myself from. While I have always had a profound connection to land, I realize that I benefit more from its existence than it does from me. In the decades since I participated in geologic fieldwork mapping basalt flows, I have undergone erosion of my own adherence to whiteness as property in the settler state. Through this, I have been fortunate to develop a reflexive praxis for further work interrogating science practices and pedagogy. Presentation of past geologic analyses, for the purposes of this paper, are woven into the examination of the erasure and forced removal of Indigenous peoples from the Shoshone-Bannock tribes who have resided in there for centuries.

I would like to acknowledge that I write this paper while sitting upon the ancestral lands of the Shoshone, Ute, and Paiute tribes. I also acknowledge and respect the past, present, and future of the Shoshone-Bannock tribes whose knowledge and relation to land is more than any geologic analysis thus far has offered.

Interstitial Latices of People and Land

Fractionation is the process that minerals within a magma chamber undergo as they cool and crystallize. As each subsequent mineral is removed from the chamber, the overall concentration of the chamber is altered as well. The initial concentration of the chemical constituents within the parent melt (that is, the pre-existing crust that was melted initially) changes with each solid particle's extrusion onto the surface. As such, an igneous petrologist could examine the solid remnants of such an extrusion and examine the changing chemistry of each step of the fractional crystallization.

The geologic evolution of the Snake River Plain in what is currently considered the state of Idaho is associated with the passage of the North American continental plate over a mantle hotspot. This geologic process formed a time-transgressive volcanic province that advanced and continues to advance in age from northeast to southwest. As the North American continental plate moved, whatever existed on the surface at the time was replaced systematically by basaltic flows of varying mafic and felsic concentrations—that is, variations in dark and light-colored minerals of respective densities. Dark (more dense) minerals crystallized first, later to be replaced by a lattice of lighter (less dense) crystals.

Settler colonialism functions in a similar way in that pre-existing peoples and cultures are systematically fractionated and replaced by those who perceive themselves as superior and deserving of the land and its resources. Not only do settlers intend to displace Indigenous peoples but also to erase their presence from the land. Total erasure, however, cannot occur. Despite the effort to completely erase, previous markings on the land will persist. Much like a palimpsest describes the still visible marks left after erasing pencil on paper, the land is a palimpsest for those who dwell on it. Therefore, though Indigenous peoples may be altered or displaced, their originality is maintained both on the land and in thousands of years of ancestral knowledge. Such is the case in melted crustal rocks extruding through fractionation, as well as the systematic relocation (like that of the Yellowstone hotspot) of the Shoshone-Bannock people eastward to the Fort Hall Reservation in southeastern Idaho.

In delivering a new methodology for "reading" the land, geologists ensure that imperial colonization maintains its superior stance in the views of the white majority of the settler state. Though methods for reading the land have been thoroughly discussed in Indigenous culture and stories for thousands of years, one aim of settler colonialism is to continually erase, alter, and replace those methodologies for those that are hegemonic in their constructions. Science as an empirical enterprise, intent on one correct answer supported by observable facts, disallows space for other ways of reading the land and its usefulness to humankind.

Geologic and Indigenous Palimpsests

> They saw themselves, and their descendants see themselves, as the true and authentic patriots, the ones who spilled rivers of blood to secure independence and to acquire Indigenous lands—gaining blood rights to the latter and they left bloody footprints across the continent. (Ortiz, 2015, p. 54)

This westward movement of conquest and violence that left bloody footprints is a violent parallel to the movement of the North American continental plate over the Yellowstone Hotspot over the last 20 million years. In a sick twist of humor, the mark left by the plate movement resembles a broad smile across southern Idaho in what is referred to as the Snake River Plain.

Prior to the arrival of European-American colonizers to the Snake River Plain in the early 1800s, the Shoshone and Bannock tribes partnered with one another to collect local plants, fish for salmon in the Snake River, and to hunt bison. The Shoshone used horses to travel and hunt, and the Bannock were skilled tradespeople. Upon the arrival of the first settlers, the Shoshone-Bannock way of life began to change. Settlers were seeking resources for economic gain, and they found the western Snake River Plain to be abundant in animals such as bison and beavers, which were hunted for their skins. Growing demand for these skins led to an increased demand on the part of the settlers for land. This also meant that there were fewer resources for the Shoshone-Bannock people. They had no choice but to participate in trade and land deals with the increasing number of settlers. Eventually these deals turned violent and the Shoshone-Bannocks' interactions with the American cattlemen shifted to actively trying to retain their homelands. Such wars had been occurring throughout the American west, and this was one of the final attempts by Indigenous peoples to keep their land and fight off the colonial intent to settle and consume resources. By 1863, the Shoshone-Bannocks instead ended up on a reservation hundreds of miles to the east known as Fort Hall (Johnson, 2011).

Historian Gregory Smoak (2006) describes the continuous forceful takeover of the settler colonists as "pivotal to Shoshone and Bannock history as the 'crystalliz[ation]' of the Bannock image as hostile and oppositional to federal Indian policy, as well as how it sharpened increasing factionalism between and within Fort Hall bands." Continual physical and legal assaults by colonists resulted in a reduction of land from which the Shoshone-Bannocks derive their existence. Over a million acres was allocated to them at Fort Hall was reduced to approximately 50,000 acres and later divided into 100-acre plots that were managed by the state of Idaho (SBtribes, 2021). Similar to how a magma chamber starts out with a vast distribution of chemical constituents, with every piece that is removed, the concentration of certain chemicals is reduced if not depleted altogether. Consequently, the Shoshone-Bannocks were left to starve without access to the plant, animal, and water resources necessary for their survival. As rivers were dammed for hydroelectric power, the waters warmed and changed the salmon habitat. As water was rerouted for agricultural needs, the camas plant that the Shoshone-Bannock relied on was no longer abundant. The wild grasses were replaced by potato and sugar beet crops, which drove the bison elsewhere for food. Not only had the Shoshone-Bannocks been forced off their land to the Fort Hall reservation, but then the reservation land was fractionated out and sold to white settlers for industrial farming.

Johnson (2011), a historian, states of colonizing forces, "Perhaps the infinitely massive energy beneath the geological and hydrological forces of the region cannot be incised from the immense personal and spiritual forces that drive some to take the drastic actions of war" (p. 10). Like the successive basalt flows over the years, waves of colonists occupied the land surface, diverted waterways, and permanently altered the region. Despite the Shoshone-Bannock nation's efforts to ward off invasion by burgeoning settler nation states, their way of life and land was eroded by greater forces than they could overcome.

14 million years prior, a different kind of settlement was forming. The thin continental crust of what is now North America was being invaded by a magma hotspot from below. As the hotspot pooled beneath the continent, magma was forced upward and into small chambers within the crust. As the liquid magma moved, it melted the pre-existing rock surrounding it, which resulted in an ever-changing concentration of mineral composition. As the liquid rock began to cool, the denser minerals solidified first and sank downward. With each mineral that crystallized, the concentration in the magma chamber was reduced to the least dense, felsic minerals. As the magma erupted onto the land surface, the minerals that had already solidified maintained their stratification from most to least dense in an upward direction, leaving the least dense, lightest colored mineral at the top.

Because of this pattern of fractional crystallization and subsequent cooling, geologists can look at old lava flows and infer what the concentration of the initial magma chamber was, as well as the crustal rocks that were melted as the magma rose to the surface. The pre-existing land surface is no longer visible or chemically present as it once was. However, chemical analyses of basalt flows indicate what had to be present on the surface in order for what is currently there to exist. It is like a geological palimpsest in that what existed previously can never be fully erased. Patrick Wolfe (2006) argues that "settler colonialism destroys to replace" (p. 388). Much like a magma flow melts pre-existing local rock to form its own rock that takes over the land surface, colonists invade Indigenous lands with the intention of staying and permanently altering what was previously there. Through the westward movement of multifarious and haphazard colonizers driven by "Manifest Destiny" ideology, settlers purloin and indelibly alter lands in a westward track across the North American continent.

Palimpsests of Land, Mind, and Body

Igneous petrologists use a machine called an Inductively Coupled Plasma Mass-Spectrometer (ICP-MS) to examine major and trace element concentrations in igneous rocks. Data gathered from these tests can indicate the precise timing of each mineral's solidification, the magnetic polarity at the time, as well as the isotopic concentration of light rare-earth elements. Essentially, the

ICP-MS indicates the fingerprint of a rock sample at the exact moment it was formed. Using these data, igneous petrologists can plot element concentrations against one another to determine the source magma concentration and the previously existing local rock that was transected. The point of which would be to backward model the basalt flow to the point where it began. Other than comparing chemical concentration to determine the original source of the magma, there really is no other purpose for this work. However, scientists like things to be predictable. Particularly, igneous petrologists like to know how and why rocks formed and subsequently changed to appear as they do to us today.

This work can be colonizing in nature. Geologists, in doing fieldwork, are expected to move upon the land surface with a particular objective, which is often their sole focus. If they are to examine a particular basalt flow, they do so regionally and then microscopically. They determine the direction of flow and any pre-existing faulting and fracturing that occurred. Then they focus on the crystal lattice of the solidified rock, and may ignore the physical presence in land and bones of pre-existing people. In the case of the basalt flow in western Idaho, they examine the concentration of dark minerals (mafic) to light minerals (felsic) and the lattice of rock between them.

The words used to describe the various generations of magma flow are curious, to say the least. The original magma inside the magma chamber is called the "primitive melt." That is, prior to crystallization. With each subsequent mineral that is crystallized out, the concentration of the remaining melt is "normalized" to its current mineral constituents. This use of language is similar to the words colonists use to describe Indigenous peoples. They have been described as "savage" and "primitive." Attempts to colonize included forceful assimilation through Indian boarding schools wherein native people were expected to shed their culture in exchange for adapting to whiteness. That is, they were expected to "normalize." That geologists use these words may be coincidental, but it is worth examining if for nothing else than to raise awareness for how geologic work can be colonizing in nature.

Wolfe (2006) states, "the logic of elimination can include officially encouraged miscegenation, the breaking-down of native title into alienable individual freeholds, resocialization in [institutions], and a whole range of cognate biocultural assimilations" (p. 3). Science and the settler colonial mindset that accompanies it seeks to dissect Native bodies, to delineate just how "native" they are, and to determine the degree to which they can be controlled or made to assimilate. If assimilation is the end goal, then, the so-called magma chamber of blood lineage in the United States would fractionate out the mafic (dark) minerals until only the felsic (white) minerals remained.

No matter how many ICP-MS measurements are run, geologists (unless, perhaps, they are Indigenous) will never have the hermeneutic understanding of land and body that Indigenous peoples do. Even if it was a land that has since been colonized and assaulted, the constituents of this land, water, and sky are embedded in the lattice of life that upholds its native peoples. Like a viscous basalt flow, "the peculiarity of settler colonialism is that the goal is elimination of Indigenous populations in order to make land available to settlers" (Wolfe, 2006, p. 388). After at least a hundred years of conquest, the Indigenous land base in the United States has been reduced to 2.3 percent of its original size (Echo-Hawk, 2011). Even if the #landback movement were to be successful, in what condition is the land being returned to its original inhabitants?

The #landback movement has four overarching goals: to dismantle white supremacy, to defund the systems that enforce white supremacy, to return all public lands back to Indigenous hands, and to seek consent for land usage rather than consultation. Ortiz (2015) suggests that "Indigenous peoples offer possibilities for life after empire, possibilities that neither erase the crimes of colonialism nor require the disappearance of the original peoples colonized under the guise of including them as individuals" (p. 235). It is as though the Indigenous palimpsest upon the land can never truly be erased, and despite the subsequent flows of colonialism, the original constituents remain.

What, then, would #landback actually look like? Lene M. Johannessen (2012), suggests we "think expansively beyond what is known about the relations between the social and the symbolic" (p. 869). That is, in terms of a palimpsest of land and its many iterations, we must also examine the palimpsests of our brain, body, and spirit. If geologists maintain a unidirectional gaze outward toward the rocks, seeking a subjectivized presence, what, then, would a gaze resemble if seeking instead an absence? Johannessen posits "the idea that processes that set out to destroy and erase actually preserve resonates powerfully with the postcolonial palimpsest" (p. 872). In other words, in addition to the returning of land to its people, we may also shift the notion in our minds of erasure to that of preservation and resurrection. Johannessen states,

> Tentatively we may at this point suggest that excavations and expositions of the sediments that constitute the palimpsest can serve as a tool as well as a metaphor for how hybridity in turn can be calibrated according to its various nuances. The more densely sedimented the textural site, the "thicker" the description, and the more accurate our assessment of cultural and political rate of exchange can be. (p. 882)

Johannessen's metaphor for land + society as a palimpsest suggests the need for hybridizing a postcolonial future. In other words, it is not simply a matter of who owns the land, but what is done upon the land with the notion of agency for all involved. In addition to that, all participants must also keep present and contend with (as the land does) a violent history of slavery, colonization, racism, and white supremacy. All land inhabitants must find "moments of confluence" (Johannessen, 2012, p. 881) in which new routes upon the previously deposited sediment may be forged. It is in the new fissures and cracks of hardened basalt that new pedagogies of land and society may occur. Because land is a place of continual change and thus permanent potential, a study of land should suggest that a postcolonial future is possible. In other words, the practice of studying land can create the transition space wherein counter-hegemonic constructions of society emerge. Johannessen (2012) calls these the sediments that constitute the palimpsest. The thicker the sediment, the denser the potential for examination into our violent histories and postcolonial futures.

Tuck and Yang (2012) state, "When metaphor invades decolonization, it kills the very possibility of decolonization; it recenters whiteness, it resettles theory, it extends innocence to the settler, it entertains a settler future" (p. 3). While I may not be able to separate myself from the notion of settler futurity due to my positionality as a white cis-woman in academia, I do recognize that movement nonetheless can occur away from the notion of land as property and toward the notion of land as learning and life. In a settler colonial quest for land resources, a disruption occurs within Indigenous relationships to the land. And this "represents a profound epistemic, ontological, cosmological violence [that is] reasserted each day of occupation" (Tuck & Yang, 2012, p. 5). Henceforth, a true #landback process is less likely to occur than a restructuring of the way settler colonial mindsets insist upon controlling the land. The movement, instead, must occur inside the structures that maintain that settler futurity. Those who maintain settler futurity must instead upend our current educational system that celebrates colonialism and erases Indigeneity. We must call home the Indigenous peoples that have been displaced through this erasure and listen to their creation stories. We must center these stories in our curriculum and erase instead the lies that portray Native peoples as a thing of the past, frozen in time. We must redefine ourselves as immigrants to this land and respect the laws and beliefs of those who occupied these lands first.

The key is desettling, in many senses of the word. Settler colonists must be made to feel desettled in a land that is not theirs. Harris (1993) speaks of land as property as follows:

> Although the Indians were the first occupants and possessors of the land of the New World, their racial and cultural otherness allowed this fact to be reinterpreted and ultimately erased as a basis for asserting rights in land. Because the land had been left in its natural state, untilled and unmarked by human hands, it was "waste" and, therefore the appropriate object of settlement and appropriation. (p. 1721)

This seems to be a backward way of viewing land. To introduce a settler mindset is to then turn it to a waste. With each movement of settler colonialism, the original purity of the land gets fractionated out. When land is untouched by human hand it is not a "waste" but instead a place of sovereignty and wholeness. It is here where scientific studies fall short.

Perennial Processes and Anti-Colonial Educational Futurity

Matter can never be created or destroyed. This is a basic tenet of scientific studies. It is absurd to think the opposite for groups of people. "Any disruption in Indigenous land, place, or culture clearly has a potentially harmful effect on Indigenous health and wellness, which may then persist for generations to come" (Walters, 2011, p. 171). Indigenous people have been fractionated, eroded and deposited since white settler-colonization began on the North American continent. Colonization is a process that is ongoing, both in action and in attitude.

When magma erupts onto the land surface, it not only melts what rocks already exist there, but it also assimilates these rocks into its evolving concentration. These rocks are altered, unrecognizable in their original form, and yet their chemical constituents remain a palimpsest upon the land. It is akin to settler colonial capitalistic disregard for the land, flippant extraction of resources, and sustained displacement of native peoples. This process results in a continued degradation and continually fractionating hope of returning the land to its original state and original inhabitants. Like a scripted palimpsest, however, the stories and energies of tribes like the Shoshone-Bannock continue to fill in the interstitial spaces between the fractionated crystals of colonization. It is only if we examine every element, present and past, that the land may tell the whole story.

One avenue of movement toward desettling the association of land with property is through land education, of which geology is a part. What if, instead of focusing our gaze on something for which we have already formed a conclusion we instead shift the gaze back onto ourselves to determine how it is we got here in the first place? What can the process of examining fractional crystallization schemes teach us about how we occupy space and time? Cajete (1999) states, "Indigenous literally means being so completely identified with a place that you reflect its entrails, its insides, its soul." Through that understanding, to examine the land is to also examine its native people and their connection to it. To examine the land separate from its people is to omit sections of data that may change the story a scientist tells.

If land is to be respected and celebrated as our teacher and part of our souls, then we must pay close attention to the lessons the land offers. Geology is the study of continual change; of erosion, deposition, eruption, solidification, and constant movement. Instead of examining rocks for the economic and property capital they offer, we can instead turn to the lessons inherent in concepts like fractional crystallization and how they offer us a new way of thinking about power and what gets destroyed as it is enacted. We must consider how we occupy space and how this is influenced by a settler-colonist mindset of what is to be considered exclusive property. Calderón (2014) suggests how land education can move place-based education forward, "especially its potential for centering Indigeneity and confronting educational forms of settler colonialism" (p. 1). Scientific endeavors often aim to name and categorize land features within a hierarchy of potential value to imperial possession and consumption. Indigenous notions of land as pedagogy, instead, can offer a view of human relationship to land as a commitment to protection and an acknowledgment of land as an agentic entity. These lessons must be centered in our science curricula, and students must be taught the truth of how violent settler-colonial practices have shaped the settler state we exist in today. If the study of basalt flows has taught me anything, it is that geologic forces may cause widespread destruction, but within the layers of deposition we can begin to understand our past and hope for a different future.

References

Cajete, G. (1999). "Look to the mountain": Reflections on indigenous ecology. In G. Cajete (Ed.), *A people's ecology: Explorations in sustainable living* (pp. 1–20). Clear Light Publishers.

Calderon, D., Lees, A., Swan Waite, R., & Wilson, C. (2021). "Crossing the bridge": Land education teacher professional development. *Professional Development in Education, 47*(2–3), 348–362. https://doi.org/10.1080/19415257.2021.1891957

Calderon, D. (2014). Speaking back to manifest destinies: A land education-based approach to critical curriculum inquiry. *Environmental Education Research, 20*(1), 24–36. https://doi.org/10.1080/13504622.2013.865114

Dunbar-Ortiz, R. (2015). An Indigenous Peoples' History of the United States (Vol. 3). Beacon Press.

Echo-Hawk, W. R. (2011). In the courts of the conqueror: The 10 worst Indian law cases ever decided. *Choice Reviews Online, 48*(08). https://doi.org/10.5860/choice.48-4666

Harris, C. I. (1993). Whiteness as property. *Harvard Law Review, 106*(8), 1721–1722. https://doi-org.ezproxy.lib.utah.edu/10.2307/134178Idaho

Johannessen, L. M. (2012). Palimpsest and hybridity in postcolonial writing. In *The Cambridge history of postcolonial literature* (pp. 869–902). Cambridge University Press. https://doi.org/10.1017/chol9781107007031.008

Johnson, S. R. (2011). *Newe Country: Environmental degradation, resource war, irrigation and the transformation of culture on Idaho's Snake River Plain, 1805–1927*. University of Nevada.

Located on the Fort Hall Indian Reservation. Shoshone-Bannock Tribes. (2021, June 14). http://www.sbtribes.com/

Smoak, G. E. (2006). *Ghost dances and identity: Prophetic religion and American Indian ethnogenesis in the nineteenth century.* University of California Press. The Constitution of the United States, Article VI, Section 1, Clause 2.

Tuck, E., & Yang, K. W. (2012). Decolonization is not a metaphor. *Decolonization: Indigeneity, Education & Society, 1*(1), 1–40.

Tuck, E., McKenzie, M., & McCoy, K. (2014) Land education: Indigenous, post-colonial, and decolonizing perspectives on place and environmental education research. *Environmental Education Research, 20*(1), 1–23. https://doi.org/10.1080/13504622.2013.877708

Walters, K. L., Beltran, R., Huh, D., & Evans-Campbell, T. (2011). Dis-placement and Disease: Land, place, and health among American Indians and Alaska natives. In L. Burton, S. Matthews, M. Leung, S. Kemp, & D. Takeuchi (Eds.), *Communities, neighborhoods, and health. Social disparities in health and health care* (Vol. 1, pp. 163–199). Springer. https://doi.org/10.1007/978-1-4419-7482-2_10

Wolfe, P. (2006). Settler colonialism and the elimination of the native. *Journal of Genocide Research, 8*(4), 387–409. https://doi.org/10.1080/14623520601056240

· 7 ·

NEITHER HERE NOR THERE: GRADUATE STUDENTS NAVIGATING THE COMPLEXITIES OF MOTHERSCHOLARSHIP DURING COVID-19

Maureen W. Nicol and Abby C. Emerson

We met during the foundational theory course for our education doctoral program. Our friendship grew when Maureen shared with Abby, who was a mother of two, that she was expecting her first child. The friendship extended beyond our shared academic interests as we talked often and regularly during COVID-19, after hours, after classes, and about our personal lives. We imagined intentional and perhaps political ways of mothering our children (Emerson et al., 2021).

By design, Eurocentric, patriarchal academic institutions were historically never intended for women to inhabit and thrive. As graduate student motherscholars (Matias, 2011), we have obligations to our children, courses, roles as instructors, CV-building projects, and maybe, for a lucky few, to our personal lives (CohenMiller & Demers, 2019; Lapayese, 2012). In our conversations we discussed where mothering and studenting intertwined, the stresses and joys in mothering generally and in graduate school specifically. Often the simultaneity of these identities, especially when layered with race, class and gender, are framed as detrimental to each other.

As COVID-19 upended our lives in New York City, we relocated closer to our families for childcare support during our studies. Motherscholars "drive the feminist impulse to dismantle patriarchal binaries—namely, the sharp divide between the intellect and the maternal, the public and the private" (Lapayese, 2012, p. 17) and we wondered about our peers who also resist these binaries. Motherscholarship is already a large task and COVID-19 only heightened it. In turn, we designed a visual exploration to understand how motherscholars are maneuvering our multiple roles, identities, demands, and desires amid COVID-19. We ask, How can the liminal spaces of our identities be used as tools to dismantle the master's house?

We utilized participant-generated visual methodologies (Drew & Guillemin, 2014) and invited motherscholars to share a photo and a vignette articulating their experiences. Presented here is an analysis of a small slice of the data. Including ourselves, we had 10 participants[1] in total. The group was diverse. Racially, we had Black, Latinx, and white motherscholars. There were seven doctoral and three masters students. Seven had parenting partners and three were single mothers. The family income ranges spanned from below the poverty line to over $150,000/year. Despite this diversity, there were consistent themes across our experiences.

The nepantla frame has been helpful in understanding how motherscholars are experiencing the pandemic. Nepantla, as theorized by Anzaldúa (2000): "I try to theorize unarticulated... lived in between overlapping and layered spaces of different cultures and social and geographic locations of events and realities—psychological, political, spiritual, historical, creative, imagined..." (p. 176). This frame helps articulate a "liminal space... the interface space between all the worlds" (Anzaldúa as cited in Keating, 2009, p. 6) In other words, nepantla describes a space of multiplicities, of in between, of being neither here nor there.

The pressure of multiple demands across our lives as motherscholars was consistent (CohenMiller, 2018). We were happy to have this unique and invaluable time with our children, but we also felt tension as we were pulled to do schoolwork. The vignettes told a story of mothers who felt this time was especially "hectic," "taxing," and "lonely." We felt "essentially chained" by what was asked of us and an overall lack of support as we sought to provide for ourselves and our families while pursuing our academic dreams. Multiple mothers talking about "stealing moments." One mother wrote, "I have to steal moments when I can to remain hopeful and focused on the goal

Figure 7.1. Mothering, working, nursing, sleeping (barely).

of graduation and finding a good job," and another wrote, "During the day I mother the best I can, stealing a few minutes here and there to write an email."

While there was a feeling of frustration in this time where we were forced to "steal moments" as if they were not ours, it was a transformative time. It forced us to understand and define our identities as mothers and scholars in new ways because the borders had dissolved (Anzaldúa, 2000). We were between spaces, desires, and emotions. This perpetual state of nepantla invited us to think in complex ways—about mothering *and* scholarship and the interplay between the two.

Drawing upon the visual collection, we learned that motherscholars have the potential to reshape patriarchal assumptions of how academic teaching and learning is done. Many of the images show us working with our children fully present (Figures 7.1 and 7.2). The images illustrate an arch of emotions, but maybe speak to the capitalistic pressure placed on women—the need to (re)produce and publish. When we were gathering data, the pandemic was raising questions: do we rest or continue the status quo? Motherscholars discussed yearning for two possibilities that seemed within reach: the desire to continue academic work and a desire to savor these times with family. The pandemic created time and space for these to seem like options, but perhaps not simultaneously.

Figure 7.2. Mothering, commenting, bathing, caring.

The white patriarchal model that imagines academics as reading and writing alone, disconnected from the world is far from our experiences—both before and during the pandemic. The capitalist trope of the superwoman mother who can "do it all" is problematic, unrealistic, and leaves participants to "feeling like [we were] failures." Our lived experiences in the academy illustrate how institutions expect women to thrive with little to no resources socially, emotionally, and financially while pursuing higher education degrees. Institutions continue to do harm every time they admit scholars without deeply considering the holistic support needed to parent, research, and connect with community. To consider these areas where support could be given also means to consider what it could mean for motherscholars to experience moments of ease—it means to reimagine motherscholars not as supermoms who can do it all, but as people who have many demands that need support, encouragement, and community.

These traditional depictions of scholars and mothers create norms that must be dismantled. By exploring our complex roles, identities, demands, and desires, we see our experiences of being neither here nor there not as a disadvantage, but an asset (Tuck, 2009). Echoing the words of the participating mothers, we wonder here how we can "steal moments" or create new realities in the academic context. Nepantla is a transformative space, and we hope that our unique positions can encourage institutions to welcome a more connected scholar, one in close community with others. We also wish that mothers were not rewarded with pats on the back for "doing it all," but given actual support.

This might look like affordable and accessible quality childcare. Or perhaps an education institution like ours could have a child-friendly space on campus for those times when we want or need to bring our children to campus with us. What would a child-friendly classroom look like? Our identities as both mothers and scholars can be a tool to carve away at the normative way academia has always been done. Again and again, we turn toward the idea of community and togetherness, eschewing the isolation we are supposed to endure as future academics. Our institutions often ask us to educate them about our needs, but the needs of mothers have been said already in many forums. Yet, little changes. Institutions, professors, and those in higher education need to make a concerted effort to build community among students if they want to support motherscholars. This will benefit motherscholars to be sure, but it will also benefit all students. We see our experiences in this pandemic time as a tool to reimagine the possibilities for community. We also know that these tensions existed before the pandemic, and we wonder what motherscholars could be if we had the support, systems, and time available to us to chip away at this deeply isolating place. Just imagine the dismantling and disruption that could be.

Note

1 Several other mothers expressed interest in participation but given the demands on their time they were not able to.

References

Anzaldúa, G. (2000). *Interviews/entrevistas*. Routledge.

CohenMiller, A. S. (2018). Creating a participatory arts-based online focus group: Highlighting the transition from DocMama to Motherscholar. *Qualitative Report, 23*(7), 1720–1735.

CohenMiller, A. S., & Demers, D. (2019). Conflicting roles of mother and academic? Exploring the use of arts-based self-care activities to encourage wellbeing. *Art/Research International: A Transdisciplinary Journal, 4*(2), 611–645.

Drew, S., & Guillemin, M. (2014). From photographs to findings: Visual meaning-making and interpretive engagement in the analysis of participant-generated images. *Visual Studies, 29*(1), 54–67.

Emerson, A., Cofield, J., & Nicol, M. (2021). Parenting as political acts of love and resistance. *Journal of Critical Thought and Praxis, 10*(2), 1–15.

Keating, A. (2009). Introduction: Reading Gloria Anzaldúa: Reading ourselves ... complex intimacies, intricate connections. In A. Keating (Ed.), *The Gloria Anzaldúa reader* (pp. 1–15). Duke University Press.

Lapayese, Y. V. (2012). Mother scholar. In Y. V. Lapayese (Ed.), *Mother-scholar: Re(imagining) K-12 education* (Transgressions: Cultural Studies and Education, Vol. 85, pp. 1–10). Brill Sense Publishers.

Matias, C. (2011). *"Cheryl Matias, PhD and Mother of Twins": Counter storytelling to critically analyze how I navigated the academic application, negotiation, and relocation process.* Paper presented at the American Educational Research Association (AERA), New Orleans.

Tuck, E. (2009). Suspending damage: A letter to communities. *Harvard Educational Review, 79*(3), 409–428.

· 8 ·

INEXTRICABLY BOUND: RACIALIZED BLACKNESS AND (IL)LITERACY IN THE UNITED STATES' IMAGINARY

CoCo Massengale

Introduction

Among the most enduring legacies of the slave system in the United States is the relationship it reinforced between what it means to be Black and what it means to be literate in the popular imagination. From the inception of this country's educational system, access to formal learning generally and literacy education specifically was stratified by the propertied, the propertyless, and the property themselves (Urban et al., 2019). Laws forbidding the education of enslaved and other Black people date back to 1740 and codified the connection between racialization and the written word (Rasmussen, 2010; Smith, 1998; Williams, 2005). Many have studied the inherently political act of educating Black Americans (Butchart, 1988; Givens, 2020; Lee & Slaughter-Defoe, 2004; Perlstein, 2002). This politicization has its roots in race-based capitalism, the maintenance of which requires the subjugation of Black people (Baptist, 2016; Collins, 1998; Robinson, 2000; Watkins, 1993). After the legal event of emancipation, the pursuit of literacy continued to be central to Black American's conceptualization of freedom (Gates, 1987; Perry, 2003; Stepto, 1991), but both de facto and de jure racial discrimination ensured that the education that might facilitate this freedom would remain withheld (Rothstein, 2017; ross, 2020). New laws restricting Black access to education guaranteed the question of Black literacy would continually be posed as a problem (Butchart, 2010; Du Bois, 1903).

Today, the rhetoric around the problem of Black literacy is as persistent as ever. Educators and the public at large are told that Black children are the least likely to read proficiently regardless of income (Feister, 2010; National Center for Education Statistics [NCES], 2020c). Studies link early reading struggles with higher rates of adult illiteracy, which is in turn associated with a lower quality of life, including poorer health and higher rates of unemployment and incarceration (Christle & Yell, 2008; Easton et al., 2010; Froiland et al., 2013). This scholarship, however, fails to recognize the country's ideological and economic investment in positioning Black people as nonreaders, and continues to reify the irreconcilability of Blackness and literacy. Inundating people with alarming reports of Black illiteracy and its dire consequences reinforces long-standing myths about Black intellectual deficiency and criminality, which has extreme material consequences. Studies have repeatedly demonstrated that Black children are disproportionately identified as learning disabled and are overrepresented in juvenile detention centers (Cruz & Rodl, 2018; Sawyer, 2019; Skiba et al., 2016), inequities that further bolster the ostensible connection between Blackness and illiteracy.

This essay investigates the historical relationship between racialized Blackness and reading to challenge normative discussions of Blackness and (il)literacy. Often, policymakers and educators approach the issue as a simple matter of helping Black students develop reading-related proficiencies. Instead, I suggest that educational discourse on Black people and literacy is informed by the presumption of illiterate Blackness which systematically distorts, devalues, and denies Black literacy practices. I first explore literacy in relation to legality and extra-legality during slavery and Reconstruction, then return to the present fears of illiteracy in the context of the enduring legacy of the trans-Atlantic slave trade. Ultimately, I trouble the notion of slavery as distal history and draw a critical connection between enslavement and literacy to today's discourse surrounding Black children's reading learning and achievement. I argue that the rhetoric around Black children and reading is that of a *bound literacy*—a theorization of the relationship between racialized Blackness and the written word as irrevocably contentious and fundamentally limited by its connection to chattel slavery. The discourse of bound literacy is characterized by fears of criminality (criminalization), low achievement (intellectual inferiority), and economic cost (societal burden).

My intention in mapping the historical relationship between slavery and reading and connecting it explicitly to present-day rhetoric is not to challenge the rhetoric as false—numerous scholars have demonstrated this through decades of critical research (e.g., Baker-Bell, 2020; Coles, 2019; Ladson-Billings, 1992; Richardson, 2003). In this essay, I am disinterested in proving Black literacy or advocating for more expansive definitions of literacy to be included into our current education system. Following the lead of Barrett (1995) as well as Flores and Rosa (2015), I am instead attempting to denaturalize our understanding of literacy to expose the racialized ideologies underlying its conceptualization. This work theorizes bound literacy as a means of disruption, ending with a consideration of the potential for an unbound literacy to elucidate alternative communicative, institutional, and broader societal possibilities.

Literacy in Education Research

The origins of much contemporary literacy research informing current policy can be traced to the work of educational developmental psychologists who understood learning as exclusively or primarily a cognitive process (Cole & Engeström, 1993; Gleitman & Rozin, 1977). Studies in alignment with developmental psychology center cognition, pedagogical approaches, and the acquisition of skills related to print literacies, with little if any regard for local or broader sociocultural contexts. These are the studies that inform the larger national literacy discourse. For example, an oft-cited article on literacy acquisition, describes the *Matthew effect* in which children—referred to as "organisms"—born into "biologically unlucky" circumstances emerge as "unskilled reader[s]" and, despite intervention, never achieve proficiency (Stanovich, 2009). Focusing on the science of reading such as the development of phonological awareness and phonemic segmentation, this study along with a host of others (e.g., Alexander-Passe, 2015; Brunner, 1993; Council of State Governments, 2015) does not mention racial disparities nor race at all. This color-evasiveness (Annamma et al., 2017) is typical of a trend in literacy studies that leverages neuroscience and "brain-based learning" to bolster reading achievement and explain discrepancies in skill development as measured by testing (e.g., Alferink & Farmer-Dougan, 2010; Hoge, 2002; Sprenger, 2013). Brain-based research builds on the same developmental psychology informing literacy studies that privilege individual cognition over alternative explanations for apparent differences.

In contrast, decades of critical literacy studies have attempted to shift the focus from individual cognition to larger societal systems and structures. Critical literacy research is especially attentive to the ways hegemony structures literacy teaching and evaluation of learning (Perry, 2012). In addition to offering a critique of literature that overemphasizes cognition and development, critical literacies explore literacy practices that empower and subvert (Morrell, 2009). Elaine Richardson's book *African American Literacies* (2003) highlighted the tension of mainstream literacy research for Black students specifically, identifying "the ideology of White supremacist and capitalistic-based literacy practices that undergird curriculum construction and reproduce stratified education and a stratified society, that reproduce the trend of African American literacy underachievement" (p. 8). Beyond a critique of the White supremacist logics informing discussions of Black achievement, Richardson explores alternate or additional literacies rooted in Black epistemologies, including Black feminism and survival. From this work, literacy researchers have explored—among many other topics—the potential of Black masculine literacies, the development of critical consciousness through subversive literacy in oppressive schools, the role of literacy in Black girls' positive identity formation, and the creation of critical race English education (Johnson, 2018; Kelly, 2020; Kirkland & Jackson, 2009; Price-Dennis et al., 2017). Using a framework that prioritizes Black literacies, education scholars have examined out-of-school literacy practices and offered counternarratives to those of illiteracy and reading underperformance that dominate mainstream discussions of reading achievement (Coles, 2019; Kinloch et al., 2017).

Research on Black literacies continues to be essential for the support of Black teachers and Black children in schools. This paper is indebted to the ongoing work of these scholars who challenge the status quo and highlight the vitality of Black literate life. Unfortunately, despite decades of this critical research, the central conversation at both the policy and practitioner levels continues to center fears of illiteracy. The theorization of bound literacy contextualizes those contemporary fears as part an unbroken lineage of U.S. slavery. I am working to describe more fully the challenge facing researchers, policymakers, and practitioners–that the construction of (il)literacy in the hegemonic U.S. imaginary has always been inextricably tied to the construction of Blackness. It is my hope that articulating this relationship will assist those of us committed to confronting antiblackness in education by rejecting bound literacy rhetoric and collectively working toward a not-yet-known future.

Conceptualizing Literacy and Blackness

The primary concepts operationalized in this paper are *literacy* and *Blackness*, which I articulate as antagonistic in the U.S. imaginary. People have been reading and writing for millennia, but the concept of literacy as a symbol of consciousness and cultural advancement is understood in academia to be a product of Modernity (Anderson, 2006; Kaestle, 1985). I use *Modernity* to connote a specific period in which industrialization, capitalism, and individualism became the governing principles of the European nations that colonized peoples on every inhabited continent (Gilroy, 1993). In this context, the Church—the vehicle of power providing both the resources and justification for the first colonial endeavors—was instrumental in the development of technologies of print, making both the Bible and theological writings more widely available and increasing the supply of written knowledge and the demand for readers (Anderson, 2006; Kaestle, 1985). By the end of the 17th century, the widespread availability of printed documents in Western Europe materially delineated the learned elite from the "ignorant" masses (Barrett, 2014; Hudson, 1994). Literacy has many meanings, but the focus here is print literacies (reading and writing) which came to prominence during Modernity and continue to be the measures of academic achievement today.

Concurrent with the development of literacy was the invention of race. Racialization signified difference and arranged people hierarchically according to constructed categories as part of the larger project of colonization characterized by the rapacious consumption, reproduction, and accumulation of global resources (Cooper, 2005; Wolfe, 2016). European colonizers assigned Blackness to the phenotypically darker indigenous peoples of Africa who "would be constructed as the ultimate referent of the 'racially inferior' Human Other" (Wynter, 2003, p. 266). In this limiting assignment, Blackness occupies the position antithetical to Whiteness: the abnormal, the uneducable, the inhuman. After superimposing a narrow conceptualization of humanity onto colonized and enslaved populations, the absence of print literacies was one of the many justifications for the violences of colonialism into the 20th Century (Barrett, 2014). The association between this understanding of Blackness and illiteracy is a central concern of this essay.

Progress and Stagnation in Education

The social sciences generally and perhaps education research particularly insist on history as merely relevant, understanding the passage of time as a linear movement toward a more progressive future. In contrast, other disciplines—particularly those aligned with Black intellectual traditions—often articulate a nonlinear conceptualization of time in which "revolutions can and often do turn backward and occur with interrupted irregularity" (Hine, 2014, p. 13). This perspective interprets contemporary Black experiences through the lens of slavery and its afterlives (Hartman, 2008; Sharpe, 2016; Walcott, 2021). Increasingly, education scholars are unsettling ideas of a clear delineation between the past and present to make sense of the lives of Black people in schools (ross, 2020; Shange, 2019; Turner, 2020). This research grapples with the embedded contempt for Blackness that pervades U.S. education (Dumas, 2016). Fundamental to this essay is the crucial intervention temporal nonlinearity may offer into the study of literacy.

Literacy, Legality, and the Making of a Mythic Illiterate Black Population

Virtually ubiquitous in present-day education discourse is what Graff and Duffy (2017) term the *Literacy Myth*, or "the belief, articulated in educational, civic, religious, and other settings, contemporary and historical, that the acquisition of literacy is a necessary precursor to and invariably results in economic development." This myth simultaneously reflects print literacies' origins (and its attendant association with the Modernist values of rationality, morality, and so on) and ignores systemic barriers (e.g., racism, classism, etc.) impeding economic and social advancement (Graff, 1994). For enslaved Africans and their descendants, literacy has never been an uncomplicated direct line to prosperity. From the beginning, literacy for Black people has been disfigured by its association with criminalization, acts of physical and psychological violence, and subjugation. Below I examine the threats Black literacy presented to both enslaved people and Whites during slavery and its immediate aftermath to trace the process through which the White ruling class systematized illiterate Blackness in the U.S. imaginary.[1]

Literacy and Slavery

The first legal regulation of Black literacy was the 1740 South Carolina Negro Act which decreed that "the having of Slaves taught to write or suffering them to be employed in writing may be attended with great Inconveniences" and would therefore be punishable by a fine for anyone offering writing instruction to enslaved persons (Goodell, 1853, p. 319). This statute did not emerge spontaneously. It was the legal response to the Stono Rebellion the previous year during which more than 90 enslaved Black people—led by their literate peer Jemmy suspected of having read anti-slavery propaganda—liberated themselves, appropriated firearms, set multiple buildings ablaze, and killed around 20 settlers before falling to the local militia (Rasmussen, 2010; Thornton, 1991). The South Carolina Negro Act codified the belief that Black literacy was both a physical and economic threat to the slave aristocracy. The statute served as the blueprint for subsequent laws throughout what would become the United States, each explicitly prohibiting teaching enslaved people to write and soon after barring reading instruction (Smith, 1998; Span, 2005). Even in places where Black literacy was not forbidden, schools in Northern states like New York were legally racially segregated, and funding for Black schools was severely limited or nonexistent (Rury, 1983). So-called free states like Connecticut also legally restricted the literacy instruction of formerly enslaved people to discourage the migration of runaways (Span, 2005). Ignoring their own antiblack policies, Northern Whites opposed Southern anti-literacy laws in ways "motivated less by concern for slaves than by pride in New England's vaunted culture of education" and "usually served to dramatize the disparity between literate cultures in the two sections of the country" (Hager, 2013, p. 34). This stance reified a belief echoed in contemporary education literature still weaponized against Black people today: illiteracy is synonymous with degeneracy (Graff, 1977).

Anti-literacy laws and related legislation were ultimately in service of maintaining the power of the White ruling class. As in the case of the Stono Rebellion and the Nat Turner Rebellion in 1831, laws in Southern states were often created to quell revolt. Narratives from formerly enslaved people confirm that literacy played a pivotal role in many stories of self-liberation. Famously, Frederick Douglass (2016) and Harriet Jacobs (2009) both used their illegally acquired abilities to read and write to escape bondage and evade recapture respectively. But there countless similar examples in both documented narratives and family lore (Barrett, 1995; Gundaker, 2007). The mythos of self-liberation through literacy was pervasive in enslaved communities and laid the foundation for what Stepto (1991) articulates as "freedom for literacy and literacy for freedom"—a concept Perry (2003) christens Black America's "indigenous and operative philosophy of learning and schooling" (p. 13). Literacy was deeply intertwined with the struggle to obtain freedom of both mind and body. While legal repercussions (e.g., imprisonment and flogging) for offering literacy instruction to those in bondage were primarily limited to White people and free Blacks, enslaved people caught reading or writing could be punished severely, typically through physical mutilation (Barrett, 1995; Grant, 2020). Despite the real threat of bodily harm, first-hand accounts from numerous formerly enslaved persons detail an irrepressible struggle to become literate while living in bondage (Cornelius, 1983). While not the focus here, the relationship between Black liberation through the written word alludes to a parallel understanding of Blackness as compatible with literacy explored further in this essay's conclusion.

Maintaining the Artifice of an Illiterate Black Population

The danger literacy represented for Whites was both physical and existential: if Black people engaged with the written word, it would offer disconfirming evidence of Black intellectual inferiority that would threaten the position of Blackness in the larger society. One justification for enslavement was the belief that people of African descent were not intelligent enough to participate in White society (Baynton, 2016). Paradoxically, this reasoning often validated the denial of literacy, creating a self-fulfilling prophecy in which Black people who were barred from reading were also believed to be unable to learn to read (Span & Anderson, 2005). Thus, while thousands of enslaved and free Black people acquired literacy nationwide (Cornelius, 1983; Johnson, 2015; McHenry, 2002; Rury, 1983), it was essential for the maintenance of the slave system that Whites *believe* Black people were incapable of literacy. Barrett (1995) captured well the ideological importance of these constraints: "to prohibit African Americans from literacy is equivalent, in terms of social organization, to proscribing African Americans from the highest realms of value and the hierarchical constructs leading to them" (p. 423). Societal subjugation of Black people was largely predicated on the presumption of illiterate Blackness.

The legal event of emancipation did not significantly impact the relationship between Blackness and literacy in the U.S. imaginary. After 1865, the ruling class continued to extralegally restrict Black people from reading and writing in former slave states. White people verbally and physically harassed Black pupils, firebombed and otherwise destroyed Black schoolhouses, and murdered Black teachers (Butchart, 2010). As during slavery, the myth of Black illiteracy was central to the preservation of the political and economic system from Reconstruction through Jim Crow. An illiterate Black workforce guaranteed the supply of cheap labor—and continued free labor through the convict leasing system—to help "rebuild" the South (Blackmon, 2009; Du Bois, 1903). Politically, literacy was frequently the litmus test for civic participation—in many states, one could not legally register to vote let alone hold political office without proof of literacy (Cascio & Washington, 2014). The suppression of literacy during slavery, the repression of Black education, and the antiblack weaponization of reading and writing at the end of chattel slavery served to confirm the perception of a perpetually illiterate Black population.

Literacy in the Wake of Slavery

The Thirteenth Amendment ostensibly ended the legal practice of slavery—with the glaring and extant exception of prisoners—in April of 1864, though it would be another 14 months until Texas would fall and be forced to release some 45,000 enslaved people. This, history tells us, is when and where slavery finally ends. Yet, today, Black people land at or near the bottom of every quality-of-life indicator. In the context of education, Black children are disproportionately identified as learning disabled, are most likely to be retained, suspended, or expelled at any age, and face the highest rates of incarceration (Cruz & Rodl, 2018; NCES, 2019a; Rovner, 2017). Black children have the second-highest high school attrition rate and second-lowest graduation rates, and Black young adults have the lowest college graduation rates (NCES, 2019b, 2020b, 2020d). These outcomes epitomize what Hartman (2008) terms the *afterlife of slavery* in which "Black lives are still imperiled and devalued by a racial calculus and a political arithmetic that was entrenched years ago" characterized by "skewed life chances, limited access to health and education, premature death, incarceration, and impoverishment" (p. 6). The afterlife of slavery offers a lens for understanding the seeming contradictions between the passage of time and the stagnation of social and economic progress for Black people. Sharpe (2016) further explicates slavery's afterlife in her concept of *wake work*, or scholarship that attends to both the dead and the living given the reality of trans-Atlantic slavery and its ongoing consequences. In this section, I consider literacy in the wake of slavery organized around three central fears: low achievement (intellectual inferiority), criminality (criminalization), and economic cost (societal burden).

Low Achievement/Intellectual Inferiority

More than 150 years after abolition, Black people continue to be seen as nonreaders, struggling readers, reluctant readers, and similar deficit labels that ignore the historical relationship between racialized Blackness and literacy. The dismal results for Black children and adults on national standardized tests and the attendant handwringing exemplify this rhetoric which proliferates. All this despite decades of critical scholarship that contests the tests' validity of standardized assessment of student knowledge. Studies using such assessments to measure Black literacy (e.g., Hernandez, 2011; Lesnick et al., 2010) serve as the basis for contemporary debates around reading achievement. Today, more than two years after the COVID-19 pandemic began, popular media is rife with articles and think pieces discussing standardized literacy test results which are considerably lower than previous years (Brown, 2021; Edge, 2021; Lloyd, 2021). Scholars have thoroughly detailed standardized testing's descendancy from intelligence testing, which is the direct product of eugenics research designed to "scientifically" validate the positioning of Blacks as intellectually inferior to Whites (Au, 2016; Lemann, 2000; Stoskopf, 2002). While the origins of this testing are clear, every state in this country continues to use standardized tests as a measure of student progress and the federal government administers a bi-annual nationwide assessment of "what students know and can do" (NCES, 2020a). I argue that it's precisely because of—and not in spite of—this association that results on aptitude and achievement tests dominate the public literacy discourse. Literacy in the wake of slavery means perpetuating ideas of Black intellectual deficiency using measures developed to prove exactly that inferiority. Relatedly, a growing body of science of reading literature traffics in the language of eugenics, offering "scientific" explanations for why children struggle to read by examining images of the brain while learning (e.g., Hoge, 2002; Sprenger, 2013). When the dominant narrative surrounding precisely which students are struggling is racialized, how can we assume that the brains under study are not also racialized? Color-evasive recommendations based on brains decoupled from their bodies ultimately reifies the myth of illiterate Blackness that is core to the U.S. imaginary.

Criminality/Criminalization

Pervasive in the literature is the emphasis on the relationship between illiteracy and "criminality." Significant research funding and effort have focused on articulating and validating the supposed connection between low literacy and incarceration and recidivism (Brunner, 1993; Christle & Yell, 2008; Council of State Governments Justice Center, 2015; Greenberg et al., 2007). Absent in this literature is any discussion of the long history preceding the present moment in which Black literacy and criminalization shared a perfectly causal relationship (Cornelius, 1983). Research linking illiteracy and criminality skips over centuries of the precise inverse relationship, pointing instead to Black illiteracy's threat to public safety. Ironically, despite the purported relationship between low literacy, criminality, and recidivism, prisons have some of the strictest limitations on what and when their occupants are allowed to read (Bianchi & Shapiro, 2018; Branch, 2009; Cauley, 2020). What logics justify such restrictions given the common rhetoric that "moral character, discipline and order, security, and productivity" are magically obtained through literacy (Graff, 1994, p. 45)? This apparent paradox suggests that the United States has an investment in Black illiteracy that supersedes the Literacy Myth in the collective ethos. Today this country's 2.3 million prisoners—forty percent of whom are Black—are the only legal exception to the federal abolition of enslavement, earning on average between 14 cents and $1.41 per hour while serving as the central commodity in a multi-billion dollar-generating industry (Gotsch & Basti, 2018; Sawyer, 2017; Sawyer & Wagner, 2020). Particularly given that Black people have always been overrepresented in prisons across the country (Blackmon, 2008; Davis, 2003), the widespread practice of limiting prisoners' access to books is a key feature of literacy in slavery's wake. Professed anxiety around the connection between illiteracy and criminality is simply another manifestation of the connection between Blackness and criminality in the U.S. imaginary.

Economic Cost/Societal Burden

Sometimes intertwined with the intellectual inferiority and incarceration research is the equally concerning "economic cost" rhetoric that emphasizes the financial burden of illiteracy. In 2021, the Oakland, California National Association for the Advancement of Colored People petitioned the local school board to address persistently low elementary literacy scores, particularly for Black students. Among other arguments, the petitioners claimed: "it is fiscally prudent to invest in establishing strong literacy skills early in a child's education" (p. 5). Such cost-benefit arguments are consistent with research highlighting the reportedly tremendous cost of illiteracy to the state. Examples include Cree, Kay, and Steward (2012) and Lal (2015), both of which estimate the annual cost of illiteracy in the United States to be $300 billion. Discussion of the economic cost of those labeled illiterate has a long history in this country which is, of course, associated with slavery. Common in public and legislative debates during Reconstruction was the devastating loss of capital associated with the abolition of slavery and the financial burden the "uneducated" formerly enslaved represented for the federal government (Butchart, 2010; Ransom & Sutch, 1988). Even those studies that do not find individuals categorized as illiterate to be a substantial financial burden (e.g., Weiss et al., 1994) still reproduce the dehumanizing logic that those labeled illiterate may be reduced to a price tag. The racialization of illiteracy as an inherently Black affliction means that scholarship exploring the connection between illiteracy and economic burden is in effect studying the relationship between *Blackness* and economic burden. This is the rhetoric of bound literacy, inseparable from its history with chattel slavery.

Recognizing Bound Literacy Today

To illustrate the analytic frame bound literacy provides, we can consider the recent settlement of the case of Ella T. versus the State of California (2017). In this case, students' families and several education advocacy groups sued the state for "allow[ing] children from disadvantaged communities to attend schools that are unable to provide them an opportunity to obtain basic literacy. These children do not learn to read properly, let alone to write properly . . ." (p. 1). The result of the settlement was the compulsory development of "Literacy Action Plans" for the 75 schools named in the complaint ("Settlement Implementation Agreement," 2020). The titular plaintiff, Ella T., is identified as "a seven-year-old African American student" who "was already more than two grade levels behind in literacy at the end of first grade" and "cannot spell basic words like 'paper,' 'dear,' 'need,' or 'help'" (p. 22). As proof of her failure, her response to a practice standardized test—in the form of a letter to the governor on how to improve her school—is included in the complaint.

A critical literacies approach to analyzing this case would fairly critique the deficit language used to describe Ella. Many would accurately affirm all the literacy Ella is demonstrating in her response; Ella attends a Spanish-English dual-language elementary and in her letter, she lists *piso* or floor as one of the many things in need of improvement at her school. Black language scholars might note her spellings of several words from her essay could be phonetic representation of Black speech as opposed to misspellings. Multiple literacies scholars could gesture to her creativity in using six different colored markers to compose her letter.

A bound literacy lens, however, offers a critique of the premise of (il)literacy used as a basis for the suit. Section III of the complaint argues there are "dire and far-reaching effects" of the plaintiffs' denial of literacy. It predictably includes subsections dedicated to the threats of limited educational attainment, incarceration, and unrealized economic self-sufficiency (pp. 15–17). Each subsection suggests that it is illiteracy—as opposed to systemic antiblackness—that will condemn children like Ella T. to lives at the margins of society. Understanding that this same rhetoric has been used since the ancestors of many of the plaintiffs in the complaint were enslaved shifts the focus from "failing" schools to the racialization of literacy itself.

Toward an Unbound Literacy

This essay traced the reification of the mutually reinforcing relationship between racialized Blackness and illiteracy in the U.S. imaginary, beginning with the trans-Atlantic slave trade through contemporary rhetoric about Black people's reading attainment and achievement. Through the exploration of this imperiled connection, I theorized that the prevailing education discourse is that of a bound literacy rooted in chattel slavery in which racialized Blackness and the written word are antagonists. I identified three central fears that characterize bound literacy: low achievement (intellectual inferiority), criminality (criminalization), and economic cost (societal burden).

Despite the abundance of literature on Black illiteracy and centuries of suppression, Black literacies are and always have been everywhere. The fact of Black literacy undermines the racial hierarchization of society and offers counternarratives to those that dominate the discussions of race and literacy. While bound literacy discourse obscures, distorts, and effaces these stories, hundreds of years of evidence suggest that this suppression fuels the innovation and proliferation of Black literacies. The potentiality of unbinding Blackness and (il)literacy for Black futures is tremendous, if daunting. Attaining bound literacy offers limited benefits: the perception of intellectual equality, the avoidance of imprisonment, and the ability to provide for oneself without state support. While these outcomes would be welcomed by many Black people who have suffered exceptionally under an unbroken regime of White supremacy, they pale in comparison to the radical goal of Black literacy which has always been freedom. An unbound literacy that draws on the ways Black people have navigated and do multiple literacies opens up broader possibilities, including both in expanding our ideas about who has been and can be literate and illuminating pathways the most educationally marginalized have and can take to engage with literacy in its many forms. Many scholars are already searching for, unearthing, studying, and enacting literacies unbound by the limitations of chattel slavery. Some of this is recovery work—bringing to light the alternate and parallel histories in which Black people were readers and writers. Some of this is resistance work—documenting and articulating the ways reading, writing, and other literacies liberate Black people from bondage. And, of utmost importance, some of this is reverie work—continuing to dream of freedom and imagine what meaning literacy might have, if any, in a free Black future.

Note

1 I use the concept of the imaginary as defined by Cornelius Castoriadis (1997) in which the imaginary is a society's ethos or "the unceasing and essentially undetermined (social-historical and psychical) creation of figures/forms/images, on the basis of which alone there can ever be a question of 'something'. What we call 'reality' and 'rationality' are its works" (p. 3). While a society may contain infinite imaginaries, here imaginary refers to the ethos of the hegemonic culture in the United States.

References

Alexander-Passe, N. (2015). Investigating post traumatic stress disorder (PTSD) triggered by the experience of dyslexia in mainstream school education?. *Journal of Psychology & Psychotherapy*, 5(6), 1–10.

Alferink, L. A., & Farmer-Dougan, V. (2010). Brain-(not) based education: Dangers of misunderstanding and misapplication of neuroscience research. *Exceptionality*, 18(1), 42–52.

Anderson, B. (2006). *Imagined communities: Reflections on the origin and spread of nationalism.* Verso Books.

Annamma, S. A., Jackson, D. D., & Morrison, D. (2017). Conceptualizing color-evasiveness: Using dis/ability critical race theory to expand a color-blind racial ideology in education and society. *Race Ethnicity and Education*, 20(2), 147–162.

Au, W. (2016). Meritocracy 2.0: High-stakes, standardized testing as a racial project of neoliberal multiculturalism. *Educational Policy*, 30(1), 39–62.

Baker-Bell, A. (2020). *Linguistic justice: Black language, literacy, identity, and pedagogy*. Routledge.

Baptist, E. E. (2016). *The half has never been told: Slavery and the making of American capitalism*. Hachette UK.

Barrett, L. (1995). African-American slave narratives: Literacy, the body, authority. *American Literary History, 7*(3), 415–442.

Barrett, L. (2014). *Racial Blackness and the discontinuity of western modernity*. University of Illinois Press.

Baynton, D. C. (2016). Disability and the justification of inequality in American history. In L. Davis (Ed.), *The disability studies reader* (5th ed., pp. 177–133). Routledge.

Bianchi, E., & Shapiro, D. (2018). Lock up, shut up: Why speech in prison matters. *John's Law Review, 92*(1), 1–28.

Blackmon, D. A. (2009). *Slavery by another name: The re-enslavement of black Americans from the Civil War to World War II*. Anchor.

Branch, K. (2009). What no literacy means: Literacy events in the absence of literacy. *Reflections, 9*(3), 52–74.

Brown, D. (2021). Crucial third grade reading scores dropped while schools and districts struggled in the pandemic. *Florida Phoenix*. Retrieved from https://www.floridaphoenix.com/2021/06/23/crucial-third-grade-reading-scores-dropped-while-schools-and-districts-struggled-in-the-pandemic/

Brunner, M. S. (1993). *Reduced recidivism and increased employment opportunity through research-based reading instruction*. National Institute of Justice, Office of Justice Programs, U.S. Department of Justice. Retrieved from https://files.eric.ed.gov/fulltext/ED361646.pdf

Butchart, R. E. (1988). "Outthinking and outflanking the owners of the world": A historiography of the African American struggle for education. *History of Education Quarterly, 28*(3), 333–366.

Butchart, R. E. (2010). *Schooling the freed people: Teaching, learning, and the struggle for black freedom, 1861–1876*. University of North Carolina Press.

Cascio, E. U., & Washington, E. (2014). Valuing the vote: The redistribution of voting rights and state funds following the voting rights act of 1965. *The Quarterly Journal of Economics, 129*(1), 379–433.

Castoriadis, C. (1997). *The imaginary institution of society*. MIT Press.

Cauley, K. (2020). Banned books behind bars: Prototyping a data repository to combat arbitrary censorship practices in US prisons. *Humanities, 9*(4), 131.

Christle, C. A., & Yell, M. L. (2008). Preventing youth incarceration through reading remediation: Issues and solutions. *Reading & Writing Quarterly, 24*(2), 148–176.

Cole, M., & Engeström, Y. (1993). A cultural-historical approach to distributed cognition. In Salomon, G. (Ed.), *Distributed cognitions: Psychological and educational considerations* (pp. 1–46). Cambridge University Press.

Coles, J. A. (2019). The Black literacies of urban high school youth countering antiblackness in the context of neoliberal multiculturalism. *Journal of Language and Literacy Education, 15*(2), 1–35.

Collins, P. H. (1998). Intersections of race, class, gender, and nation: Some implications for Black family studies. *Journal of Comparative Family Studies, 29*(1), 27–36.

Cooper, F. (2005). *Colonialism in question: Theory, knowledge, history.* University of California Press.

Cornelius, J. (1983). "We slipped and learned to read:" Slave accounts of the literacy process, 1830–1865. *Phylon (1960–), 44*(3), 171–186.

Council of State Governments (US) Justice Center. (2015). *Locked out: Improving educational and vocational outcomes for incarcerated youth.* Council of State Governments Justice Center. Retrieved from https://csgjusticecenter.org/wp-content/uploads/2020/01/LOCKED_OUT_Improving_Educational_and_Vocational_Outcomes_for_Incarcerated_Youth.pdf

Cree, A., Kay, A., & Steward, J. (2012). *The economic and social cost of illiteracy: A snapshot of illiteracy in a global context.* World Literacy Foundation. Retrieved from https://worldliteracyfoundation.org/wp-content/uploads/2021/07/TheEconomicSocialCostofIlliteracy-2.pdf

Cruz, R. A., & Rodl, J. E. (2018). An integrative synthesis of literature on disproportionality in special education. *The Journal of Special Education, 52*(1), 50–63.

Davis, A. Y. (2003). *Are prisons obsolete?.* Seven Stories Press.

Douglass, F. (2016). *Narrative of the life of Frederick Douglass, an American slave.* Yale University Press.

Du Bois, W. E. B. (1903). *The Souls of Black Folk: Essays and sketches.* A. C. McClurg.

Dumas, M. J. (2016). Against the dark: Antiblackness in education policy and discourse. *Theory Into Practice, 55*(1), 11–19.

Easton, P., Entwistle, V. A., & Williams, B. (2010). Health in the "hidden population" of people with low literacy. A systematic review of the literature. *BMC Public Health, 10*(459), 1–10.

Edge, S. (2021). Spring reading scores down from pre-pandemic levels. *Idaho Ed News.* Retrieved from https://www.idahoednews.org/news/spring-reading-scores-down-from-pre-pandemic-levels/

Ella T. vs. the State of California, C.A. County of Los Angeles. (2017). Retrieve from https://media2.mofo.com/documents/171205-ellla-t-v-california-complaint.pdf

Fiester, L. (2010). *Early warning! Why reading by the end of third grade matters. KIDS COUNT special report.* Annie E. Casey Foundation. Retrieved from https://assets.aecf.org/m/resourcedoc/AECF-Early_Warning_Full_Report-2010.pdf

Flores, N., & Rosa, J. (2015). Undoing appropriateness: Raciolinguistic ideologies and language diversity in education. *Harvard Educational Review, 85*(2), 149–171.

Froiland, J. M., Powell, D. R., Diamond, K. E., & Son, S. H. C. (2013). Neighborhood socioeconomic well-being, home literacy, and early literacy skills of at-risk preschoolers. *Psychology in the Schools, 50*(8), 755–769.

Gates, Jr., H. L. (1987). *Figures in black: Words, signs, and the "racial" self.* Oxford University Press.

Gilroy, P. (1993). *The black Atlantic: Modernity and double consciousness.* Harvard University Press.

Givens, J. R. (2020). Literate slave, fugitive slave: A note on the ethical dilemma of Black education. In C. A. Grant, A. N. Woodson, & M. J. Dumas (Eds.), *The future is Black: Afropessimism, fugitivity, and radical hope in education* (pp. 22–31). Routledge.

Gleitman, L. R., & Rozin, P. (1977). The structure and acquisition of reading I: Relations between orthographies and the structure of language. In A. S. Reber, & D. L. Scarborough (Eds.), *Toward a psychology of reading: The proceedings of the CUNY conference* (pp. 1–54). Lawrence Erlbaum.

Goodell, W. (1853). *The American slave code in theory and practice: Its distinctive features shown by its statutes, judicial decisions, and illustrative facts.* American and Foreign Anti-Slavery Society. Retrieved from https://quod.lib.umich.edu/m/moa/ABJ5059.0001.001?view=toc

Gotsch, K., & Basti, V. (2018). Capitalizing on mass incarceration US growth in private prisons. The Sentencing Project. Retrieved from https://www.sentencingproject.org/wp-content/uploads/2018/07/Capitalizing-on-Mass-Incarceration.pdf

Graff, H. J. (1994). Literacy, myths and legacies: Lessons from the history of literacy. In L. Verhoeven (Ed.), *Functional literacy: Theoretical issues and educational implications* (pp. 37–60). John Benjamins Publishing Company.

Graff, H. J. (1977). "Pauperism, misery, and vice"; Illiteracy and criminality in the nineteenth century. *Journal of Social History, 11*(2), 245–268.

Graff, H. J., & Duffy, J. (2017). Literacy myths. In B. Street & S. May (Eds.), *Literacies and language education. Encyclopedia of language and education* (3rd ed.). Springer. Retrieved from https://doi.org/10.1007/978-3-319-02252-9_4

Grant, C. A. (2020). Radical hope, education, and humanity. In C. A. Grant, A. N. Woodson, & M. J. Dumas (Eds.), *The future is Black: Afropressimism, fugitivity and radical hope in education* (65–71). Routledge.

Greenberg, E., Dunleavy, E., & Kutner, M. (2007). *Literacy behind bars: Results from the 2003 National Assessment of Adult Literacy Prison Survey* (NCES 2007–473). National Center for Education Statistics. Retrieved from https://files.eric.ed.gov/fulltext/ED496564.pdf

Gundaker, G. (2007). Hidden education among African Americans during slavery. *Teachers College Record, 109*(7), 1591–1612.

Hager, C. (2013). *Word by word: Emancipation and the act of writing.* Harvard University Press.

Hartman, S. (2008). *Lose your mother: A journey along the Atlantic slave route.* Macmillan.

Hernandez, D. J. (2011). *Double jeopardy: How third-grade reading skills and poverty influence high school graduation.* Annie E. Casey Foundation. Retrieved from https://assets.aecf.org/m/resourcedoc/AECF-DoubleJeopardy-2012-Full.pdf

Hine, D. C. (2014). A black studies manifesto: Characteristics of a black studies mind. *The Black Scholar, 44*(2), 11–15.

Hoge, P. T. (2002). *The integration of brain-based learning and literacy acquisition.* Georgia State University.

Hudson, N. (1994). *Writing and European thought 1600–1830.* Cambridge University Press.

Jacobs, H. A. (2009). *Incidents in the life of a slave girl: Written by herself, with "A true tale of slavery" by John S. Jacobs.* Harvard University Press.

Johnson, A. (2015). A class all their own: Economic and educational independence of free people of color in Antebellum Louisiana. In D. Danns, M. A. Purdy, & C. M. Span (Eds.), *Using past as prologue: Contemporary perspectives on African American educational history* (pp. 33–56). Information Age Publishing.

Johnson, L. L. (2018). Where do we go from here? Toward a critical race English education. *Research in the Teaching of English, 53*(2), 102–124.

Kaestle, C. F. (1985). The history of literacy and the history of readers. *Review of Research in Education, 12*, 11–53.

Kelly, L. L. (2020). Exploring Black girls' subversive literacies as acts of freedom. *Journal of Literacy Research, 52*(4), 456–481.

Kinloch, V., Burkhard, T., & Penn, C. (2017). When school is not enough: Understanding the lives and literacies of Black youth. *Research in the Teaching of English, 52*(1), 34–54.

Kirkland, D. E., & Jackson, A. (2009). "We real cool": Toward a theory of black masculine literacies. *Reading Research Quarterly, 44*(3), 278–297.

Ladson-Billings, G. (1992). Liberatory consequences of literacy: A case of culturally relevant instruction for African American students. *The Journal of Negro Education, 61*(3), 378–391.

Lal, B. S. (2015). The economic and social cost of illiteracy: An overview. *International Journal of Advance Research and Innovative Ideas in Education, 1*(5), 663–670.

Lee, C. D., & Slaughter-Defoe, D. T. (2004). Historical and sociocultural influences on African American education. In J. A. Banks (Ed.), *Handbook of research on multicultural education.* Wiley.

Lemann, N. (2000). *The big test: The secret history of the American meritocracy.* Macmillan.

Lesnick, J., Goerge, R., Smithgall, C., & Gwynne, J. (2010). *Reading on grade level in third grade: How is it related to high school performance and college enrollment.* Chapin Hall at the University of Chicago. Retrieved from http://citeseerx.ist.psu.edu/viewdoc/download?doi=10.1.1.715.5162&rep=rep1&type=pdf

Lloyd, D. (2021). STAAR math, reading score declines in Cy-Fair ISD reflect statewide trends. *Community Impact Newspaper.* Retrieved from https://communityimpact.com/houston/cy-fair/education/2021/06/28/staar-math-reading-score-declines-in-cy-fair-isd-reflect-statewide-trends/

McHenry, E. (2002). *Forgotten readers: Recovering the lost history of African American literary societies.* Duke University Press.

Morrell, E. (2009). Critical research and the future of literacy education. *Journal of Adolescent & Adult Literacy, 53*(2), 96–104.

National Center for Education Statistics. (2019a). *Digest of Education Statistics 2017, Indicator 15: Retention, suspension, and expulsion.* United States Department of Education. Retrieved from https://nces.ed.gov/programs/raceindicators/indicator_rda.asp

National Center for Education Statistics. (2019b). *Integrated postsecondary education data system (IPEDS), Spring 2002 through Spring 2013 and Winter 2013–14 through Winter 2018–19, Graduation Rates component; and IPEDS Fall 2012, Institutional Characteristics component.* United States Department of Education. Retrieved from https://nces.ed.gov/programs/digest/d19/tables/dt19_326.10.asp

National Center for Education Statistics. (2020a). *About NAEP: A common measure of student achievement.* United States Department of Education. Retrieved from https://nces.ed.gov/nationsreportcard/about/

National Center for Education Statistics. (2020b). *Public High School Graduation Rates.* United States Department of Education. Retrieved from https://nces.ed.gov/programs/coe/pdf/2021/coi_508c.pdf

National Center for Education Statistics. (2020c). *Results from the 2019 Mathematics and Reading Assessments*. United States Department of Education. Retrieved from https://www.nationsreportcard.gov/mathematics/supportive_files/2019_infographic.pdf

National Center for Education Statistics. (2020d). *Status Dropout Rates*. United States Department of Education. Retrieved from https://nces.ed.gov/programs/coe/pdf/2021/coj_5 08c.pdf

Oakland Branch of the National Association for the Advancement of Colored People. (2021). *Administrative petition for improved literacy in Oakland Public Schools*. Retrieved from https://speakerdeck.com/acoach/administrative-petition-for-improved-literacy-in-oakland-public-schools

Perlstein, D. (2002). Minds stayed on freedom: Politics and pedagogy in the African-American freedom struggle. *American Educational Research Journal, 39*(2), 249–277.

Perry, K. H. (2012). What s literacy? A critical overview of sociocultural perspectives. *Journal of Language and Literacy Education, 8*(1), 50–71.

Perry, T. (2003). Up from the parched earth: Toward a theory of African-American achievement. In T. Perry, C. Steele, & A. Hilliard (Eds.), *Young, gifted, and black: Promoting high achievement among African-American students* (pp. 1–108). Beacon.

Price-Dennis, D., Muhammad, G. E., Womack, E., McArthur, S. A., & Haddix, M. (2017). The multiple identities and literacies of black girlhood: A conversation about creating spaces for black girl voices. *Journal of Language and Literacy Education, 13*(2), 1–18.

Ransom, R., & Sutch, R. (1988). Capitalists without capital: The burden of slavery and the impact of emancipation. *Agricultural History, 62*(3), 133–160.

Rasmussen, B. B. (2010). "Attended with great inconveniences": Slave literacy and the 1740 South Carolina Negro Act. *Pmla, 125*(1), 201–203.

Richardson, E. (2003). *African American literacies*. Routledge.

Robinson, C. J. (2000). *Black Marxism: The making of the Black radical tradition*. University of North Carolina Press.

ross, k. m. (2020). Black space in education: (Anti) Blackness in schools and the afterlife of segregation. In C. A. Grant, A. N. Woodson, & M. J. Dumas (Eds.), *The future is Black: Afropressimism, fugitivity and radical hope in education* (pp. 47–54). Routledge.

Rothstein, R. (2017). *The color of law: A forgotten history of how our government segregated America*. Liveright Publishing.

Rovner, J. (2017). Still increase in racial disparities in juvenile justice. *New Amsterdam Times*.

Rury, J. L. (1983). The New York African free school, 1827–1836: Conflict over community control of Black education. *Phylon (1960–), 44*(3), 187–197.

Sawyer, W. (2017). How much do incarcerated people earn in each state? Prison Policy Initiative. Retrieved from https://www.prisonpolicy.org/blog/2017/04/10/wages/

Sawyer, W. (2019). Youth confinement: The whole pie 2019. Prison Policy Initiative. Retrieved from https://www.prisonpolicy.org/reports/youth2019.html

Sawyer, W., & Wagner, P. (2020). Mass incarceration: The whole pie 2020. Prison Policy Initiative. Retrieved from https://www.prisonpolicy.org/reports/pie2020.html

"Settlement Implementation Agreement," C.A. County of Los Angeles (2020). Retrieved from https://media2.mofo.com/documents/200220-literacy-ca-ella-t-settlement-agreement.pdf

Shange, S. (2019). *Progressive dystopia: Abolition, antiblackness, and schooling in San Francisco.* Duke University Press.

Sharpe, C. (2016). *In the wake: On blackness and being.* Duke University Press.

Skiba, R. J., Artiles, A. J., Kozleski, E. B., Losen, D. J., & Harry, E. G. (2016). Risks and consequences of oversimplifying educational inequities: A response to Morgan et al. (2015). *Educational Researcher, 45*(3), 221–225.

Smith, H. L. (1998). Literacy and instruction in African American communities: Shall we overcome?. In B. Pérez (Ed.), *Sociocultural contexts of language and literacy* (pp. 189–222). Taylor & Francis.

Span, C. M. (2005). Learning in spite of opposition: African Americans and their history of educational exclusion in antebellum America. *Counterpoints, 131,* 26–53.

Span, C. M., & Anderson, J. D. (2005). The quest for "book learning": African American education in slavery and freedom. In A. Hornsby, Jr., (Ed.), *A companion to African American history* (pp. 295–311). Blackwell.

Sprenger, M. B. (2013). *Wiring the brain for reading: Brain-based strategies for teaching literacy.* Wiley.

Stanovich, K. E. (2009). Matthew effects in reading: Some consequences of individual differences in the acquisition of literacy. *Journal of Education, 189*(1–2), 23–55.

Stepto, R. B. (1991). *From behind the veil: A study of Afro-American narrative.* University of Illinois Press.

Stoskopf, A. (2002). Echoes of a forgotten past: Eugenics, testing, and education reform. *The Educational Forum, 66*(2), 126–133.

Thornton, J. K. (1991). African dimensions of the Stono Rebellion. *The American Historical Review, 96*(4), 1101–1113.

Turner, D. C. (2020). Making the world go dark: The radical (im)possibilities of youth organizing in the afterlife of slavery. In C. A. Grant, A. N. Woodson, & M. J. Dumas (Eds.), *The future is Black: Afropressimism, fugitivity and radical hope in education* (pp. 107–116). Routledge.

Urban, W. J., Wagoner, J. L., & Gaither, M. (2019). *American education: A history.* Routledge.

Walcott, R. (2021). *The long emancipation: Moving toward Black freedom.* Duke University Press.

Watkins, W. H. (1993). Black curriculum orientations: A preliminary inquiry. *Harvard Educational Review, 63*(3), 321–338.

Weiss, B. D., Blanchard, J. S., McGee, D. L., Hart, G., Warren, B., Burgoon, M., & Smith, K. J. (1994). Illiteracy among Medicaid recipients and its relationship to health care costs. *Journal of Health Care for the Poor and Underserved, 5*(2), 99–111.

Williams, H. A. (2005). *Self-taught: African American education in slavery and freedom.* University of North Carolina Press.

Wolfe, P. (2016). *Traces of history: Elementary structures of race.* Verso Books.

Wynter, S. (2003). Unsettling the coloniality of being/power/truth/freedom: Towards the human, after man, its overrepresentation—An argument. *CR: The New Centennial Review, 3*(3), 257–337.

· 9 ·

HOW CAN I TEACH ANTIRACISM IN MY ALL-WHITE CLASSROOM? A CALL TO WHITE TEACHERS

Julia Kingsdale, Scout Cohen-Pope, and Cynthia Benally

Evidence increasingly indicates the necessity of addressing bias and hate both societally and in schools. In 2018, the FBI reported that personal attacks based on bias and prejudice reached their highest reported numbers in 16 years (Hassan, 2019), and those numbers jumped yet again in 2020, increasing by more than 13 percent (U.S. Department of Justice, 2020). The Department of Justice has determined that the majority of these hate crimes are motivated by "race/ethnicity/ancestry bias." Sadly, hate crimes at K-12 schools have also risen sharply. Most of these incidents are motivated by racism, followed closely by homophobia and xenophobia (Costello & Dillard, 2019).

Despite the efforts of *Brown v. Board*, schools in the United States remain highly segregated by race (Frankenberg et al., 2019). White students are more segregated than other racial groups, as they frequently attend majority-white schools; the typical white student is likely to attend a school that is nearly 70% white (Frankenberg et al., 2019). Furthermore, tracking practices within schools tend to segregate students by race. Consequently, white students may find themselves in classrooms that are skewed even more heavily white than school-level data indicate (Lewis & Diamond, 2015). In addition, approximately 80 percent of teachers in the United States are white (National Center for Education Statistics, n.d.). Given this pattern of de facto racial segregation in our schools, as well as the growing numbers of race-based hate crimes both within and outside of schools, antiracist curricula explicitly designed to be implemented by white teachers in majority-white classrooms are urgently needed.

We are three educators (two white in-service teachers and a Native tenure-track professor) who endeavor to teach in anti-oppressive and decolonizing ways. Our paths crossed through a social foundations department at a primarily white institution (PWI) located in the United States. Our chapter responds to a question raised by our colleague, a white middle-school teacher, who asked, "How can I teach antiracism responsibly in my all-white classroom in a predominantly white community?" She reported that when she raised topics of racism with her white middle-school students, they parroted superficial antiracist sentiments, yet they also demonstrated limited knowledge about communities of color and actively resisted engaging in meaningful self-reflection. Despite a climate of legislative antagonism toward Ethnic Studies programs and more general discussions of race in K-12 classrooms (speciously referred to as Critical Race Theory), this white teacher was committed to improving her antiracist pedagogy in response to her students' resistance. From our own experience as teachers; she is not alone.

Simultaneously, Cynthia, a Native professor, tried to make sense of her white pre-service teachers' pushback in a compulsory multicultural education course. Within most teacher education programs, multicultural education courses are often the only courses responsible for training pre-service teachers on curricula that include equity, diversity, and inclusion. Because the course focused on supporting K-12 students of color, the white pre-service teachers who would ultimately teach in predominantly white classrooms considered the course content irrelevant to their future practices. Although white teachers need training on how to teach students of color responsibly, Cynthia told an additional need for teacher education programs located in PWIs to prepare white teachers to teach antiracism to their future white students.

In response to these unmet needs, we decided to conduct a literature review to improve our pedagogical practices with white students and with white pre-service teachers of white students. As we present our findings, we call to mind our duty, as articulated by Laura Nader (1972), to examine "the culture of power rather than the culture of the powerless" (p. 289). With this responsibility in mind, we lovingly call in our fellow white teachers and teacher educators to critically examine the prevalence, nature, and efficacy of antiracist curricula in our predominantly white K-12 classrooms.

We began this chapter by explaining why we wanted to examine antiracist teaching practices in predominantly white classrooms. We follow with how we conducted our research and the findings from our literature review, which suggest that some antiracist curricula maintain problematic discourses on race and whiteness while others help to reframe classroom conversations around white supremacy. We end with implications for teachers/teacher educators.

Methodology

We conducted this study to gain new insight into how white teachers can teach in predominantly white classrooms in antiracist ways. Julia and Scout hoped to use the pre-existing literature to improve their antiracist teaching practices as white teachers. As a teacher educator, Cynthia was eager for insight into how to better prepare white pre-service teachers to teach antiracism in their predominantly white classrooms. We did not approach this literature review as academic researchers but as practitioners intending to improve our practices.

We surveyed peer-reviewed journal articles published between 2000 and 2020 in the following databases: Google Scholar, Ebscohost, Wiley, and the Education Resources Information Center. We used the following keywords: *K12/K-12*, *elementary school*, and *secondary school* with *antiracist/antiracism*, *curriculum/curricula*. We combined the previous keywords with *white teachers* and *white students*. We defined curriculum broadly as the content and objectives used in lesson planning and delivery. We also defined antiracist/antiracism as any attempt to address or counter racial inequities. Using the search terms, we compiled about 150 journal abstracts. We reviewed these articles to identify those that focused on white teachers teaching antiracist curricula in predominantly white classrooms (i.e., where 50% or more of the students identified as white). A shockingly low count of four research articles met all these criteria. We each read and annotated the articles, then compiled our notes to identify common themes. We intentionally limited our research to peer-reviewed publications to evaluate how antiracist pedagogies are implemented in practice and assess their efficacy. Table 9.1 summarizes the four articles we reviewed as part of this study.

Findings

While our initial research terms focused on curricula, the articles in our study emphasized antiracist pedagogy over any specific curriculum, suggesting that the art of teaching matters more than materials or resources. We found three

Table 9.1. Literature Reviewed, Including Participants and Settings

Author(s), Year, Journal	Study Participants	Study Place and Time
Christina Berchini, 2016, *Counterpoints*	A white male teacher and his ninth-grade English class at a public high school with a "predominantly white, rural student population" (p. 82).	A public high school in a "rural Midwestern town" (p. 83); timeframe not specified.
Jane Bolgatz, 2005, *Multicultural Perspectives*	One Black male teacher, one white female teacher, and 25 high school juniors and seniors who were white (18), Black (three), Chicano (one), Asian (one), and mixed race (one). The students were predominantly male and from low-income households.	A public, alternative high school in a Midwestern city during one 12-week term in the spring of 1999.
Carlin Borsheim-Black, 2015, *Research in the Teaching of English*	A white female English teacher and 26 ninth-grade students, all but two of whom identified as white.	A high-performing high school in a wealthy, predominantly white (98%) area in Michigan during six weeks of an unspecified school year.
Rebecca Rogers and Melissa Mosley, 2006, *Reading Research Quarterly*	Two white female teacher-researchers and five white second graders (two female and three male) from working-class families.	A racially and economically diverse school district in St. Louis during the 2002–2003 school year.

common themes around such pedagogy: multiple ways of engaging whiteness, strategically using texts, and taking antiracist opportunities.

Multiple Ways of Engaging Whiteness

Antiracist pedagogies engage with whiteness in complex and multifaceted ways. In the four studies we reviewed, antiracist pedagogies elicited white students to enact "hybrid discourses" of noticing, enacting, and deconstructing whiteness (Rogers & Mosley, 2006). Additionally, several studies suggested that antiracist pedagogy should consider whiteness not as a monolithic category but as an identity with diverse possibilities. Finally, white teachers working with predominantly white students presented unique opportunities for antiracist learning alongside unique limitations.

Hybrid Responses to Whiteness

In all four studies, white students responded to antiracist pedagogy by noticing, enacting, and deconstructing whiteness, a pattern described as "hybrid discourses" by Rogers and Mosley (2006). By making whiteness "more visible [and] less neutral" (Borsheim-Black, 2015, p. 416), antiracist pedagogies led white students to notice whiteness as both an individual and also a systemic phenomenon. At the individual level, some students began to identify themselves as white. Naming their race for the first time allowed them to understand white people as racialized (Rogers & Mosley, 2006). At the systemic level, many students shifted from an understanding of race and whiteness simply as phenotypic traits toward recognizing race and whiteness as socially constructed indicators of power and status (Berchini, 2016; Rogers & Mosley, 2006).

Both students and teachers enacted whiteness during their antiracist lessons. Students demonstrated a variety of tactics when enacting whiteness, including using colorblind language that minimized the experiences of racism (Berchini, 2016; Bolgatz, 2005; Borsheim-Black, 2015; Rogers & Mosley, 2006) and sidelining conversations about race to discuss their own experiences (Bolgatz, 2005; Rogers & Mosley, 2006) or to divert attention toward other social identities (Berchini, 2016; Bolgatz, 2005). Teachers sometimes enacted whiteness by avoiding "touchy" topics or examples of racism when they feared it would lead to conflict or reflect poorly on them (Borsheim-Black, 2015, p. 421). Other times, teachers reinforced whiteness when they failed to intervene in problematic discussions students were having about race, choosing to remain silent because they worried interjecting would "relieve [students] of the responsibility of examining white privilege and racism" (Rogers & Mosley, 2006, p. 479).

Finally, white teachers and students used various tactics to deconstruct whiteness during antiracist lessons. Both teachers and students critiqued the linguistic and narrative choices in texts that reinforced whiteness as the norm, such as failing to name the race of white individuals but naming race among Black individuals (Rogers & Mosley, 2006) or setting up racist white characters as heroes (Borsheim-Black, 2015). Students also began to recognize and critique white people's "unfair practices" and how these practices enabled the unequal distribution of material resources (Rogers & Mosley, 2006, p. 482).

Furthermore, students articulated how white people's understandings of race and whiteness could change and "hypothesiz[ed] about how to be an ally as a white person" (Rogers & Mosley, 2006, p. 483).

Noticing, enacting, and deconstructing whiteness did not happen in a linear progression through discrete stages (Rogers & Mosley, 2006), but rather took place dialogically, i.e., with movement back-and-forth across each discursive element and often during the same lesson or discussion. During a classroom discussion, for example, a teacher helped her students notice the way racial norms influenced their language choices while, at the same time, she and her students reinforced whiteness by articulating and accepting colorblind narratives (Borsheim-Black, 2015). In another example, a white student made a powerful statement in class that simultaneously critiqued "the economic and material privilege associated with whiteness" and reduced racism to an individual rather than a systemic phenomenon (Rogers & Mosley, 2006, p, 481).

Whiteness as an Identity with Diverse Possibilities

In two studies, the authors challenged the idea that whiteness is a monolithic identity and argued that antiracist pedagogies should treat whiteness as an identity with diverse possibilities. Rogers and Mosley (2006) emphasized the importance of teaching beyond white privilege and white supremacy. They suggested explicitly teaching what it means to be a white antiracist by providing "counter examples of the productive and powerful ways that whiteness can be used to benefit society" (p. 480). The authors argued such counterexamples could teach students that antiracism is not just the work "of heroes and heroines" of color but the work of everyone, including everyday white people (p. 480). In their study, the white teachers helped their students explore this other side of whiteness by "ask[ing] the students to place themselves in the role of a white person who is an activist against racism" (p. 482). In addition, Borsheim-Black (2015) suggested that the range of attitudes white families demonstrated in her study indicated white diversity. While some white parents made angry complaints to their school about antiracist pedagogy in their children's classroom, others appreciated that their children were learning to challenge "dominant White ideology" (p. 422). Borsheim-Black (2015) cautioned her readers not to assume a monolithic white response to antiracism, but rather to design antiracist pedagogy with "diverse and complex White racial identities" in mind (p. 422).

The concept of whiteness as a diverse identity with potential for societal good deserves scrutiny. While we agree with Rogers and Mosley (2006) about the importance of explicitly teaching white students how to be antiracist, we challenge the idea that whiteness itself carries the potential "to benefit society" (p. 480) given that whiteness is a construction of racial dominance that serves to hoard power and privilege (Bonilla-Silva, 2017; Castagno, 2014). In addition, Borsheim-Black's (2015) assertion that white identities are "diverse and complex" (p. 422) masks the fact that white people's differing responses to antiracist pedagogy often derive from a common collection of white norms (Bonilla-Silva, 2017; Castagno, 2014; DiAngelo, 2018). Furthermore, we question these authors' concern about treating white people as a "monolithic" group, given that, in the context of a nation founded on white supremacy, it is racially marginalized groups who are typically treated as monolithic. In contrast, white people are commonly treated as unique individuals. The focus on "diversity" among white people ultimately serves to center whiteness within the context of an ostensibly antiracist pedagogy.

Opportunities and Limitations for Antiracist Pedagogy in Predominantly White Classrooms

The predominantly white enrollment of the classrooms in these studies offered both opportunities and limitations for antiracist learning. Enactments of whiteness were, unsurprisingly, prominent in these classrooms, and the antiracist teachers often utilized these opportunities to interrogate whiteness in the moment (Berchini, 2016; Bolgatz, 2005; Borsheim-Black, 2015; Rogers & Mosley, 2006). In one instance, hurtful misunderstandings about race among the students in an all-white reading group were used as opportunities to learn without the risk that articulating and investigating these misunderstandings might be painful and unproductive for students of color (Rogers & Mosley, 2006). While such exploration can be extremely harmful in predominantly white classrooms that include students of color, entirely white learning groups can allow white students to articulate and unlearn problematic understandings about race (Tatum, 2017).

At the same time, whiteness often found its way back to the center of the discussions in these predominantly white classrooms. Discussions often featured a limited, white-centric point of view (Borsheim-Black, 2015), and students sometimes spoke as though to "an implied audience of other white people" (Rogers & Mosley, 2006, p. 477). In addition, the prevalence of white voices in these discussions served to privilege the experiences, thoughts, and feelings of white people (Rogers & Mosley, 2006). While teachers endeavored to make these spaces "safe" for white students to examine their whiteness (Borsheim-Black, 2015; Rogers & Mosley, 2006), these same conversations may not have felt safe for students of color. These enactments of whiteness opened the door for critical interrogation, yet they also maintained the "normalcy and centrality of Whiteness" in predominantly white classrooms (Borsheim-Black, 2015, p. 41). This tension reminds us of the ongoing debate about the merits of whiteness studies in academia, in which efforts to analyze and deconstruct whiteness also serve to recenter whiteness (Matias & Boucher, 2021).

Strategically Using Texts

White antiracist teachers used texts strategically as entry points into dialogue about race, racism, and whiteness. While some teachers handpicked texts for their antiracist content and approach, their schools or departments often also required them to use texts that contained problematic racist elements. The teachers in these studies utilized both chosen and required texts to critically explore issues of race.

Teacher-Chosen Texts

In all four studies, teachers handpicked texts that served as strategic entry points into critical conversations about race. These texts addressed race explicitly, and while some were chosen to introduce personal testimonies of racism (Bolgatz, 2005; Borsheim-Black, 2015), others examined racism on a systemic level (Berchini, 2016; Borsheim-Black, 2015; Rogers & Mosley, 2006). Many of these texts served to elicit students' emotional engagement with and critical analysis of topics of race and racism (Berchini, 2016; Bolgatz, 2005; Rogers & Mosley, 2006). In addition, these texts provided additional opportunities for students to consider the perspectives of people of color (Borhseim-Black, 2015), validating and empowering students of color in the classroom (Bolgatz, 2005).

In many instances, these teacher-chosen texts successfully guided antiracist learning. In one classroom, for example, the text "Poem For the Young White Man Who Asked Me How I, an Intelligent, Well-Read Person, Could Believe in the War Between Races" by Lorna Dee Cervantes generated a lively discussion during which students articulated and critiqued their perceptions of racism (Bolgatz, 2005). Yet not all teacher-chosen texts were able to engage students in the ways teachers intended. In another example, one teacher used Leonard Pitts Jr.'s 2012 op-ed, "Don't Lower the Bar on Education Standards," as an effective entry into discussing institutional racism, but his students resisted his efforts to interpret the article through the lens of white privilege (Berchini, 2016).

When selecting texts, white teachers need to know how their whiteness impacts their understanding of what makes a text antiracist. Therefore, we suggest white teachers prioritize antiracist texts by authors of color and ask themselves the following critical questions: Where did I find this text and why am I using it? What research drives me to choose this text?

Required Texts

In several cases, teachers were required to teach additional texts they considered problematic with respect to race, yet they used these texts strategically as part of their antiracist pedagogy. In one example, a high school English teacher was required to teach the book *To Kill a Mockingbird*, a book that "privileges a White perspective on racism," centers a narrative of white saviorism, and treats racism as "an individual issue rather than a systemic one" (Borsheim-Black, 2015, pp. 418–419). Rather than ignoring these issues or pausing her antiracist efforts, the teacher instead guided her students to critically analyze several of the text's problematic elements, including the racist attitudes of the novel's white hero. In another study, many of the guided-reading books in a unit on the Civil Rights Movement avoided naming race explicitly and failed to hold white people accountable for racist behavior (Rogers & Mosley, 2006). However, the teachers engaged with these problems by leading their students to critique the authors' and illustrators' choices (Rogers & Mosley, 2006). In both cases, the teachers demonstrated that "reading against problematic racial ideologies" in texts could serve as "a rich opportunity for antiracist pedagogy" (Borsheim-Black, 2015, p. 420). Given the prevalence of required reading lists outside individual teachers' control and the recent surge in book-banning efforts, we believe teachers must learn how to use required texts strategically to investigate issues of race and racism. The teachers in these studies provided valuable models for teaching required texts.

Creating Antiracist Opportunities

Antiracist pedagogy was either reinforced or undermined by the real-time decisions white teachers made while teaching. Teacher choices that enabled antiracist learning included asking questions to drive student discussions and reflections, exposing and interrogating enactments of whiteness within the classroom, modeling race talk, and being persistent in response to student resistance. Teacher choices that undermined antiracist learning frequently involved staying silent rather than challenging students' enactments of whiteness or raising topics of race that might elicit student resistance. In addition, white teachers made choices about how to navigate conflicts between antiracist pedagogy and student-directed learning, and these choices impacted antiracist learning in their classrooms.

Asking Questions to Drive Student Discussion and Reflection

The white teachers in these studies strategically asked questions to center and deepen students' reflections on whiteness and racism. Sometimes these questions challenged students to explore the implications of race within the context of prepared lessons. Other times these questions involved "go[ing] off on a tangent" from prepared lessons to expose and interrogate students' assumptions and experiences of race (Berchini, 2016, p. 84). For example, to respond to his students' resistance and to make explicit the ubiquity of white privilege, one teacher interrupted his lesson on racist educational policies to discuss everyday examples of whiteness that were not obvious to his students, asking questions such as "what color are flesh-colored Band-Aids? . . . what skin color does every Disney character have, except for one? . . . did you notice how every evil [Disney] character has darker skin?" to drive the discussion (Berchini, 2016, pp. 86–87). While this strategic use of questions effectively guided students to be more critical in their thinking and self-reflection around race, we also suspect that the efficacy of this approach depends on a teacher's level of preparedness to respond to resistance and misunderstanding among her students. Such preparedness requires a certain familiarity and comfort with antiracist pedagogy, yet most teacher education programs do not address these skills.

Exposing and Interrogating Enactments of Whiteness Within the Classroom

Additionally, white teachers interrupted and interrogated enactments of whiteness as they happened, creating new opportunities for antiracist learning. In one classroom, when white students used collective pronouns vaguely (e.g., "they" and "we") in a discussion, their teacher repeatedly responded with questions crafted to expose the racial assumptions embedded in their language choices (Borsheim-Black, 2015). At the same time, when teachers chose not to interrogate real-time enactments of whiteness, these choices served to undermine opportunities for antiracist learning (Borsheim-Black, 2015; Rogers &

Mosley, 2006). For example, when a white second-grade student stated that Martin Luther King, Jr. ended racism, his white teacher did not challenge this misconception but instead pushed forward with the literacy lesson (Rogers & Mosley, 2006). When these same white teachers engaged in reflections of their antiracist pedagogy, they were sometimes able to identify and articulate how their own choices had served to reinforce, rather than disrupt, their students' hegemonic understandings of race (Rogers & Mosley, 2006). As with the strategic use of questions to drive student discussions and reflections, teachers' ability to recognize, interrupt, and interrogate enactments of whiteness requires training and grounding in antiracist pedagogy that teachers rarely receive as part of their formal teacher education.

Modeling Race Talk

White teachers also supported antiracist learning among their students when they modeled how to talk explicitly, comfortably, and self-reflectively about whiteness, race, and racism. When teachers modeled being "open and at ease with what might have been seen as a delicate [racial] issue," students also felt more comfortable talking about race (Bolgatz, 2005, p. 31). Furthermore, when white teachers openly acknowledged their complicity with whiteness and racism, students built upon these acknowledgments to "challenge norms of whiteness" (Bolgatz, 2005, p. 34). Conversely, when teachers chose not to interject into conversations in which their students perpetuated misunderstandings of race and enacted whiteness, they forfeited opportunities to model "resisting white privilege and institutionalized racism" for their students (Rogers & Mosley, 2006, p. 478).

When white teachers share their own mistakes, they widen the space for white students to do the same. These demonstrations of humility, as white educator Frankie Mastrangelo (2019) explains, are an important tool "in creating the spaces we want to see and communities worth cultivating" (p. 61). Modeling also can help teachers develop greater trust with their students. "The places where you are wrong," adrienne marie brown (2017) reminds us, are often "the most fertile ground for connecting with others" (p. 85). When teachers use modeling as a form of pedagogy, they forge a path for white teachers and students to move forward together in resisting white privilege and racism.

Navigating Conflicts Between Antiracism and Student-Directed Learning

The white teachers in these studies sometimes encountered what they perceived to be conflicts between antiracism and student-directed learning; in these instances, the efficacy of their antiracist pedagogy was mediated by how they navigated these conflicts. These teachers sometimes chose not to interrupt or challenge enactments of whiteness in their classrooms because they believed doing so would limit their ability to co-construct meaning with their students. For example, a group of white second-grade students minimized Jim Crow segregation laws by suggesting that "the blacks [sic] should be happy even if they are on the back [of the bus] because at least they get to ride," and that walking is a healthier, and therefore more desirable, alternative to using public transportation (Rogers & Mosley, 2006, p. 477). The teacher did not interrupt or critique her students' comments "because she wanted to provide a safe place for the children to co-construct meaning" (Rogers & Mosley, 2006, p. 478). As another teacher explained, "I don't want to have a classroom where [the students] feel like I'm trying to make them feel a certain way, like indoctrinate them" (Borsheim-Black, 2015, p. 423). By not challenging certain enactments of whiteness and racism in their classrooms, these teachers effectively maintained what Leonardo and Porter (2010) call "white comfort zones"—spaces that prioritize white comfort over preventing or challenging racism—in the name of student-directed learning.

We believe, however, that teachers can challenge racism and still leave plenty of space to co-construct meaning with their students. For example, when whiteness is enacted in their classrooms, teachers can name how they feel and use these feelings to generate critical classroom discussions. Alternatively, they can ask probing questions that explore how whiteness is operating in the classroom. Using these and other strategies, teachers can disrupt enactments of whiteness in their classrooms without telling their students how to feel or what to think. When teachers choose to remain silent, however, they effectively "protect [white] students from reflecting on their own racism" (Borsheim-Black, 2015, p. 424). Furthermore, as Borsheim-Black argues, the desire not to "indoctrinate" one's students is antithetical to antiracist pedagogy, since all pedagogies, including traditional pedagogies, are forms of indoctrination. While traditional pedagogies reinforce hegemonic American values, such as individualism and meritocracy, as well as white supremacist perspectives on racism—perspectives that often minimize the role of race and racism in contemporary and historical society—antiracist pedagogies attempt to challenge these ideologies.

Discussion

We believe our study has important implications for K-12 teachers, teacher educators, and educational researchers. We were disappointed by how limited the research was on white teachers engaging with antiracist pedagogy with their white students. While we know antiracist teaching is not the norm among white K-12 teachers, our experiences suggest that examples of such teaching are nevertheless underrepresented within academic literature. If we want all teachers, including white teachers, to teach students antiracism, we need to be prepared to suggest and assess which pedagogical strategies work.

While the research available for our study was limited, we nevertheless noticed several meaningful patterns. Perhaps most profoundly, teacher choice appears to be a significant factor in reframing classroom conversations around racism and white supremacy. White teachers are most effective at reframing these conversations when they ask questions to drive student discussions and reflections, expose and interrogate enactments of whiteness within their classrooms, model race talk, and respond persistently and consistently to student resistance. Additionally, when confronted with real-time enactments of whiteness, teachers are responsible for choosing to interrupt and trouble their students' understanding of race and racism.

Given their central role in enacting effective antiracist pedagogy, teachers need to invest in deepening their understanding of whiteness, race, and racism. To do this, we believe white teachers must seek out antiracist texts, professional development, and membership in learning communities that engage in white identity work, critical self-reflection, and peer mentorship. We recommend white teachers reflect on their antiracist practices by interrogating their hegemonic understandings of race and by critically evaluating how their pedagogical choices reinforce or disrupt their students' understandings.

In addition, white teachers can improve their antiracist pedagogy by grounding their practice in theory. Few of the educators in these studies defined antiracism or antiracist pedagogy explicitly, and there is a danger in assuming, as white teachers, that we know how to enact or recognize antiracism. Instead, we suggest that white teachers lean on theory, especially theories developed by educators and scholars of color, rather than relying on their intuition. One theoretical framework we think might be particularly fruitful for white teachers is Abolitionism; this calls on teachers to act as co-conspirators in eradicating injustice in schools (Love, 2019).

Our study has notable implications for teacher education programs in predominantly white institutions. Upon graduating from such programs, many white teachers return to their predominantly white communities to teach in predominantly white schools, and research indicates that multicultural curricula are minimally effective in these settings (Milner, 2005). Teacher education programs can better prepare white teachers to address racism and white supremacy in predominantly white settings by offering coursework on whiteness and white racial identity development (Helms, 1995). Such coursework would require white pre-service teachers to interrogate their racial identities and analyze how whiteness upholds systemic racism. Additionally, this type of coursework would provide strategies for building communities of practice for antiracist teaching.

We hope this review can provide a starting place for white teachers looking to incorporate antiracist themes into curricula for their predominantly white classrooms. We also hope this review will help illuminate the many unlit corners that remain in the research on white teachers implementing antiracist curricula with white students and will sound a call to critical education scholars for additional research on this topic.

References

Berchini, C. (2016). "I don't think Disney has anything to do with it": Unsettling race in a white English classroom. *Counterpoints, 477*, 81–93.

Bolgatz, J. (2005). Teachers initiating conversations about race and racism in a high school class. *Multicultural Perspectives, 7*(3), 28–35.

Bonilla-Silva, E. (2017). *Racism without racists: Color-blind racism and the persistence of racial inequality in the United States.* Rowman & Littlefield.

Borsheim-Black, C. (2015). "It's pretty much white": Challenges and opportunities of an antiracist approach to literature instruction in a multilayered white context. *Research in the Teaching of English, 49*(4), 407–429.

brown, a. m. (2017). *Emergent strategy: Shaping change, changing worlds.* AK Press.

Castagno, A. E. (2014). *Educated in whiteness: Good intentions and diversity in schools.* University of Minnesota Press.

Costello, M., & Dillard, C. (2019). Hate at school. Southern Poverty Law Center. https://www.splcenter.org/sites/default/files/tt_2019_hate_at_school_report_final_0.pdf

DiAngelo, R. (2018). *White fragility: Why it's so hard for white people to talk about racism.* Beacon Press.
Frankenberg, E., Ee, J., Ayscue, J. B., & Orfield, G. (2019). *Harming our common future: America's segregated schools 65 years after Brown.* The Civil Rights Project. https://www.civilrightsproject.ucla.edu/research/k-12-education/integration-and-diversity/harming-our-common-future-americas-segregated-schools-65-years-after-brown/Brown-65-050919v4-final.pdf
Hassan, A. (2019, November 12). Hate-crime violence hits 16-year high, F.B.I. reports. *The New York Times.* https://www.nytimes.com/2019/11/12/us/hate-crimes-fbi-report.html
Helms, J. E. (1995). An update of Helm's white and people of color racial identity models. In J. G. Ponterotto, J. M. Casas, L. A. Suzuki, & C. M. Alexander (Eds.), *Handbook of multicultural counseling* (pp. 181–198). Sage Publications.
Leonardo, Z., & Porter, R. K. (2010). Pedagogy of fear: Toward a Fanonian theory of "safety" in race dialogue. *Race Ethnicity and Education, 13*(2), 139–157. https://doi.org/10.1080/13613324.2010.482898
Lewis, A. E., & Diamond, J. B. (2015). *Despite the best intentions: How racial inequality thrives in good schools.* Oxford University Press.
Love, B. L. (2019). *We want to do more than survive: Abolitionist teaching and the pursuit of educational freedom.* Beacon Press.
Mastrangelo, F. (2019). Safe(r) spaces and future cops. In J. Mink (Ed.), *Teaching resistance: Radicals, revolutionaries, and cultural subversives in the classroom* (pp. 57–62). PM Press.
Matias, C. E., & Boucher, C. (2021). From critical whiteness studies to a critical study of whiteness: Restoring criticality in critical whiteness studies. *Whiteness and Education, 8*(1), 64–81. https://doi.org/10.1080/23793406.2021.1993751
Milner, H. R. (2005). Developing a multicultural curriculum in a predominantly white teaching context: Lessons from an African American teacher in a suburban English classroom. *Curriculum Inquiry, 35*(4), 391–427.
National Center for Education Statistics. (n.d.). *National teacher and principal survey.* https://nces.ed.gov/surveys/ntps/tables/ntps1718_fltable01_t1s.asp
Rogers, R., & Mosley, M. (2006). Racial literacy in a second-grade classroom: Critical race theory, whiteness studies, and literacy research. *Reading Research Quarterly, 41*(4), 462–495.
Tatum, B. D. (2017). *Why are all the Black kids sitting together in the cafeteria? And other conversations about race.* Basic Books.
U.S. Department of Justice. (2020). *2020 hate crime statistics.* https://www.justice.gov/hatecrimes/hate-crime-statistics

· 10 ·

"BUT LOOK AT MY SIGN!" WE CRIED: AND OTHER TYPES OF WHITE PERFORMANCE THAT WILL NEVER DISMANTLE THE HOUSE

Scott D. Farver

This work is critical in calling out white allies who claim to be co-conspirators, as the poem forces us (white folks) to examine the *actual* work we are doing outside of performative pieces (that is, posting hashtags and/or sharing "inspirational" quotes on MLK day). This work in turn problematizes the normative ways that white allyship is seen within education, and in particular, places of schooling. This "allyship" often tends to focus on Black history only in the month of February; or centers the same few voices (i.e., Dr. Martin Luther King, Jr., Rosa Parks, or Harriet Tubman) in limited ways; or passes resolutions or mission statements without taking steps toward liberation. Such "slacktivism" is comforting for white folks, but leads to no action. The hope is that work such as this poem can help force us white folks working in schools to critically examine the ways we are centering and honoring Black lives within the curriculum in order to move past such limited views of allyship (e.g., "We had students write I have a Dream poems last year").

A broader goal of this poem would be that this work encourages other white "allies" *outside* of education to re-examine the ways they claim to be supportive of dismantling oppressive structures both inside and outside of education, while continuing to benefit from their continued existence—for these folks to see past the performative nature of their "support" (blacking out their social media page; sharing hashtags) to thinking about what it means to have "skin in the game," as it were. As Love (2019) reminds us, "co-conspiracy functions as a verb, not a noun" (p. 117). A goal of this work would be to offer white folks a reminder of this, as we move away from labeling ourselves and toward liberatory action.

"bUt LoOk aT My sIgN!" We Cried: And Other Types of White Performance That Will Never Dismantle the House

The Prelude, or, Considering Tense

Hughes asks
(and in fact answers himself)
What happens when
A dream
Is deferred.

What is left unsaid, unspoken,
but known to those who read these lines and nod
Having had their own dreams
Deferred
Glossed over
Overlooked by faces bathed in whiteness.

We never needed to think about
The difference between active and passive.
For we are the ones doing
The deferring.
We read and hear the passive voice
The past is the past is the past.

As if somehow,
The dream was deferred
By accident.
It just
Happened

Using our active voices
to say out loud and turn it around
That's such bad luck.

"BUT LOOK AT MY SIGN!" WE CRIED

It just so happens that a dream is deferred every once in a while.
By no one in particular.
It
Just
Happens.

And we play with the passive again
The past is the past is the past
What. Are. you. Going. To. Do?

We need to move on
Get over it.
The past is the past is the past
Grab those bootstraps and just
Pull.

But what if we stop playing with tenses?
What if we ask
A question where we
The benefactors of whiteness
Are the active subjects of interrogation?

"By whom" is a good question to start with.
By *whom* are these dreams deferred?
A verb needs a subject.
This is no accident
Or mere happenstance.
The bowl did not fall from the counter on its own
Shattering into so many pieces.

We are the bowl pushers
Shattering ourselves into pieces
By splitting apart tenses
Actively glossing over
The dignity of people whose dreams we actively defer.
Hiding our participation to the past and the present,
Fooling no one,
Only ourselves.

We
Pushers of bowls
Who see no active participant in the deferring of dreams
Continue to defer.
Actively.

Daily.
Will shrug
And tell anyone who listens

Sometimes
A *bowl is broken.*
A *dream is deferred.*
It
Just
Happens.
What. Are. you. Going. To. Do?
The *Past is the past is the past.*

The First Act, or, My House is My Castle

The master's tools
Will never dismantle the master's house.
But what if
Those tools—
The implements used over and over and over
Across the changing of seasons year after year after year,
And that house—
The sturdy walls that have
Grown stronger each season
Instead of deteriorating
Year after year after year
And crumbling from the passage of time.
Become, instead,
Stronger?

What if those tools that built the house
Used to create the condition
We find ourselves in—
What if those tools
And that house
Belong
To me?

They are mine.
When I look around
Safe and secure in the protective walls
That let me breathe
And exist freely

All five fifths of me.
I see those tools
Still stacked
Organized and alphabetized so neatly
In rows and rows and rows
Each helping me in different ways.
Protecting. Profiting. Pilfering.

These tools built the house
My house
The house I am able to live in
Thrive in

Those tools will not tear down the house
They are used to maintain it and keep the house
In perfect working order
Kept in rows and rows and rows.

The Second Act, or, The Crocodile Pleads Her Case

My desk was wet with her violence
The tears soaking everything around us.
But thankfully,
My whiteness does not feel the sting
of her perceived slights

Her tears
That had thought about making an appearance in class
But decided not to fully reveal themselves
Were not ashamed to meet me in my office.

Yeah, but,
Yeah, but,
Yeah, but,
Had been her mantra of the day
Each time a voice pleaded with her
To listen to their pain
She countered and parried

These tears are acidic
Toxic and dangerous when dropping.

Violence in liquid form.
But
In my office
With just me to witness them
There is no damage

But those tears have power
The victim card her winning Ace
Able to help her counter and parry
And weave new truth
And summon an army
To protect her

Thewordsflowincrediblyfast
Bundledtogethertoprovethepoint
Sheistryingtomake

As if another nanosecond
Of not letting me know
How good she is
Would be painful.

It's really more about class, you now?
It's in the past.
I don't own slaves.
I work so hard.
Why can't They just work hard like me?
Then the big volley
Match point.
If only They did
this or that or this or that or this or that
Them them them them they they they they

She pleaded her case
About how
Everyone should matter
Especially
People like her brother
Who patrols the mean streets of a nearby city.

That's all she meant in class.
Don't those lives matter as well?

One last deluge as

She sputtered again,
Like
About how
You couldn't even see her profile picture for a week
Like
Her Black friend from home whose name
Seems to be
Just at the tip of her tongue.
But they were really, really close.
Like
The book she ordered
Well, it's in her cart
But as soon as she gets
More money put into her account
She will definitely
Buy the book
And maybe
Read it.

Her phone appears.
To show me
To prove to me
How good she is
"bUt LoOk aT My sIgN!" she sobbed
"iT's GoInG iN mY yArD!"

The sound of her cry
Was drown out by the cacophony of safety pins
Clanging on her backpack.
As she leaves to go speak
With my Chair.

The Third Act, or, The Trouble I Have Unzipping My Own Jacket

I wear the words, I write the words. I do the work
I sometimes even
Pat myself on the back.

But walking across campus,
My zipped sweatshirt
My books in my backpack

Are hidden.

To dismantle the house is to take pieces of myself
The tools that built this castle
Are mine.
Stored in rows and rows and rows.

It is more than me wearing the words that I share
At my lectern.
Those wearing the blanket of whiteness before me
Some nodding and notetaking
Some buried in the books
or
Gazing boringly out the window
I see both at the same time.

Many students talk of love and of King and his Dream
And try to iron out the sharp corners that I lay down that push deeper.
Yeah, they want to change the world, but change
Takes
Time
You
Know?

To take down the system is too much for some to consider
They are protected
By the same white wall that surrounds me
And to take that down
Would be painful
That imagination can be hard for them

And
For me.

As I walk across campus
I get to make the choice
Of when
And how
And where
I reveal myself.
That I do this work.
That I have a sign in my own yard.

Not

All white people . . .
Would be what I might say to folks who see me
And think the worst.

But it is
All white people.

Because who else
Gets to Choose
Whether we wear the words
Or say the words
Or do the words
Or to just
Keep our jacket zipped up and walk across campus
Back to our house
With a sign in the yard?

· 11 ·

THE CRIP FUTURES OF ACADEMIC MADNESS: EDUCATION, SCHOOLING, AND THE STRUGGLE AGAINST SANISM

Sam Shelton

In this chapter, I theorize and critically examine the relationships between education and sanism, as it interacts and intersects with other systems/structures of domination, in order to better articulate what education could become through the pursuit and practice of Mad liberation. In particular, I argue that collectively dreaming and organizing toward anti-sanist worlds will require radical transformations in the ways we comprehend and practice education, because its contemporary forms too often perpetuate harmful ideas, values, and norms which make up the very foundation of Mad oppression. My intention in pursuing this line of thought is to further nuance conversations surrounding social justice education by centering an historically marginalized intellectual position grounded in lived experiences of violence and harm.

Much of my thinking in this chapter is guided, both implicitly and explicitly, by bell hooks' well-known description of education as "the practice of freedom" (hooks, 1994). I am particularly interested in the questions of who gets included in this notion of "freedom" and how educators might differently center justice frameworks and movements to promote collective liberation and "consistent anti-oppression" (Brueck & McNeill, 2020). Part of the argument I seek to develop in this chapter is that social justice education too often assumes a particular oppressed subject and prioritizes certain axes of power while marginalizing, neglecting, and/or colluding with others like sanism. And while different situations may necessitate centering, for instance, racism or capitalism, a truly intersectional or ecological[1] approach to social justice education means examining inequity and injustice in their entirety from many different angles. My chapter aims to identify opportunities to incorporate anti-sanist values/practices into social justice education, and it calls for some radical shifts in how critical educators go about our work. The interventions and transformations I explore here have the potential to both open up opportunities for solidarity with Mad peoples and to expand possibilities for pursuing freedom against other systems of dominance.

Guiding Concepts and Frameworks

Before transitioning into the main arguments of my paper, I must define some of the central concepts that inform my argument. Sanism refers to "an oppression, a belief system, and the pervasive form of violence that makes it possible for psychiatric diagnosis, medication, and other 'therapeutics' to strip away dignity and livelihood" (Meerai et al., 2016, p. 21). As a system of power, sanism disseminates normative, idealized beliefs about mental and emotional states that become a foundation for discipline and population management. Experiencing reality outside of these compulsory forms of enmindedment subjects individuals to various forms of punishment ranging from social exclusion and isolation to incarceration, institutionalization, and forced medication and "treatment" (Ben-Moshe & Carey, 2014; Kafer, 2013). If and how individuals are punished for their Madness, neurodivergence, or neuroqueerness, as well as the resources and support provided for them, depends, in large part, on their other positions within the "matrix of domination" (Collins, 1990), for the experience of sanist institutions like psychiatry is always mediated by race, class, gender, sexuality, and other sites of power and difference (Diamond, 2013). Indeed, for Mad liberation to become reality, anti-sanism must be an intersectional practice dedicated to working across and between social justice movements/frameworks (Redikopp, 2021).

Psychiatric and psychological paradigms/texts, especially the *Diagnostic and Statistical Manual of Mental Disorders*, establish a crucial basis for pathologization through which the surveillance and discipline of mental difference becomes part of the typical functioning of the carceral settler state. Pathologization, or the discursive production of psychic deviance, detracts and distracts from analyses of social inequity/injustice by obscuring the impacts of social systems on individual bodyminds. Obscuring this impact, in turn, results in violence and harm against neurodivergent, neuroqueer, and Mad peoples, who come to be seen as strange, dangerous, unwelcome rather than grounded in a specific lived reality. Moreover, the hegemony of psychology and psychiatry within academia is largely responsible for the proliferation and institutionalization of sanist belief systems (Menzies et al., 2013), and so the contents of this essay are especially relevant to critiques of education and knowledge-making. Insofar as the influence of psy disciplines has spread throughout educational space, often with limited critical attention and reflection, this conversation is relevant to multiple fields and disciplines across intellectual spaces and educational institutions.

In opposition to sanism, Madness describes an anti-pathological reclamation of mental and emotional difference centered around lived experiences and needs of the most impacted peoples (Menzies et al., 2013). Movements for Mad liberation seek to dismantle the foundations of sanism and open up space for alternative modes of togetherness rooted in consensual, interdependent, accountable relationships. Relatedly, Mad Studies is a field of critical inquiry that works to disrupt dominant schemes for making sense of "mental health"/"mental illness" in order to generate opportunities to comprehend Madness differently (Snyder et al., 2019). Mad Studies carries many queer tendencies in the sense that its scholars seek to challenge enminded normativity and unsettle disciplinary regimes, particularly those promoting sanism. The field poses critical questions that carry interdisciplinary relevance, and its scholarship and activism offer anti-pathological pathways toward intellectual and social transformation. As with many other critical disciplines, such as Women's and Gender Studies, Disability Studies, and Ethnic Studies, Mad Studies has activist roots and aspirations: it does not seek to make knowledge just for knowledge's sake, but rather to craft possibilities for organizing and resistance in response to lived experiences of sanist oppression.

Finally, the sanist construction of Madness as mental illness or deviance is intersectional, for the people most subjected to pathologization, surveillance, institutionalization, incarceration, or other harms tend to be disadvantaged along multiple axes of power. Sanist belief systems and practices are intertwined with the logics of settler colonialism, White Supremacy, neoliberal capitalism, and cisheteropatriarchy, and it is the enactment of power in relation to mental and emotional difference that forms an historical rationale for hatred and violence against most oppressed groups. Scientific racism, Social Darwinism, missionaries, and boarding/residential schools, to name a few examples, are all grounded in oppressive ideas of intelligence and mental/emotional "fitness."

White supremacy has repeatedly sought to justify itself by "proving" that people of color have lesser capacities for rationality and cognitive functioning and pathologizing people of color for refusing to accept oppressive circumstances (Meerai et al., 2016; Redikopp, 2021). Pathologization has also been weaponized against gendered subjects as demonstrated by the problematic history of conditions like Hysteria (Maines, 2014; Ussher, 2013), the fabrication of disciplinary disorders like "battered woman syndrome" (Durazo, 2006), and the denial of queer/trans people's bodily autonomy outside of psychiatric diagnosis (Spade, 2006). These and other systems of power could not operate in the same way without the co-operation of sanism, and so it is vital to center intersectionality in all conversations about Madness as well as social justice more broadly.

Mad Liberation and the Urgency of Anti-Sanist Education

In her seminal work, *Teaching to Transgress*, bell hooks (1994) argues that education can be a practice of freedom. Similar sentiments underlie most accounts of critical education, which by and large are built around the radical idea that teaching and learning can be anti-oppressive tools of intellectual liberation. Yet, the looming question remains: "To whom is this radical idea applied?" Even as many social justice educators have at least outwardly embraced the call for intersectionality, much work remains for us in terms of figuring out how to teach toward collective liberation and consistent anti-oppression. Many teachers, myself included, are faced with a difficult task of engaging students in the critical analysis of intersecting systems of power and oppression while simultaneously resisting the conditioned tendency to fall back on single-axis thinking. One of the many enduring challenges facing social justice educators is learning how to center particular oppressed groups and their struggles for liberation without further marginalizing or detracting from others—or how to focus in on specific experiences and needs without sacrificing awareness of the broader oppressive social structure in which all people are implicated. For freedom is all or nothing—it demands solidarity across social movements and struggles (Jordan, 1992; Sins Invalid, 2016; Taylor & Hunt-Hendrix, 2019).

An essential aspect of social justice education for teachers is continually questioning the ways that we are complicit in systems of power and oppression even as the guiding motive of our work is to support students in unlearning dominance so they can be more engaged in the labor of liberation and freedom

(Balén, 2005, p. 272). For if we are to remain true to ourselves and our goals, then social justice educators in particular must always be willing to reflect on our own areas for growth, admit that our teaching practices are imperfect and have more than likely caused harm, and acknowledge that unlearning and dismantling oppression is so messy that none of us can keep our hands clean. Assuming a critical stance means accepting that visions of freedom, equity, and justice we promote are inherently limited by our consciousness. We all have a partial perspective, and this simple truth of our humanity is why the labor of social justice must be collective and ongoing. But therein lies the integrity of life, for it is the partiality of our experiences and worldviews that makes us interdependent with one another. Embracing and honoring differences is the key to our collective survival, and so critical education has to begin with the comprehension of how we suppress and discipline difference through our actions in and beyond the classroom (Lorde & Hall, 2004; Sensoy & DiAngelo, 2014).

In my experience, social justice educators, especially within higher education, tend to be self-reflective up to a certain point, but struggle to truly expand or transform their perspectives. Rigidity to alternative ideas and frameworks seems to be a big part of the reason why social justice educators routinely bolster sanism and marginalize Mad students, even those participating in meaningful acts of resistance. Much of the time, I have found that the hegemony of race, class, and gender theorists limits space for critical examination of other sites of power and difference, especially ableism and sanism. This foreclosing of space is troublesome for several reasons, the most considerable of which being that White supremacy, capitalism, and cisheteropatriarchy all depend on continued violence against and hatred of embodied and enminded difference (Redikopp, 2021; Sins Invalid, 2016). In other words, without a sustained and meaningful critique of both ableism and sanism, social justice educators and students cannot fully understand how power functions to unfairly distribute life chances across multiple sites of difference. The logics of sanism, in particular, have been used to bolster every other system of oppression as they provide a socially accepted rationale for social stratification, especially since the emergence of modern concepts of sanity, rationality, and intelligence during the Enlightenment (Meerai et al., 2016; Starkman, 2013).

Despite the importance of critiquing sanist frameworks, many educational spaces, even including ones committed to principles of social justice, peddle a sanist worldview composed of problematic beliefs and assumptions about sanity, rationality, and intelligence. This worldview in turn reproduces inequity and injustice in the classroom and the broader society by teaching students to view particular forms of enmindedment as normal/desirable and others as bad, deviant, suspicious, and dangerous. Because sanism is an inherently intersectional system of oppression, sanist frameworks present in educational spaces can simultaneously function to normalize, invisiblize, and rationalize violence along other axes of power and difference, especially against people of color, queer and trans folk, women, poor people, and disabled people. Consequently, actively dismantling sanism is a crucial part of liberatory education in general, and one which all social justice educators must deliberately practice in our pedagogies. Yet, anti-sanist teaching remains elusive, for many social justice educators have not made an effort to align their/our teaching with movements for Mad liberation or with the knowledge emerging from the field of Mad Studies.

The interdisciplinary field of Mad Studies aims to problematize sanist worldviews and leave them more porous to critical questions which, in turn, create space for alternative understandings of concepts like sanity, rationality, and Madness. These alternative understandings in time establish the basis for social and relational transformation, which I understand to be a primary intention of social justice education. For example, in resistance to sanism, Mad Studies draws critical attention to the individualized medical model of "mental illness" that has become dominant across most educational institutions through the often-unchallenged authority granted to "psy" disciplines (Snyder et al., 2019). A big part of what Mad Studies ultimately works to do is generate critical intellectual space in which to explore and make sense of the ways that mental states/psychic experiences are socially constructed and, therefore, inseparable from the social arrangements shaping people's lives. This intention goes against the tendency of "psy" disciplines to medicalize and pathologize individuals as if they could be isolated from the world around them. It also connects critiques of neuronormativity together with other social justice frameworks and movements, thus furthering the ongoing project of intersectionality.

Building from the critical examination and critique offered by Mad Studies, an anti-sanist approach to social justice education generates space for teachers and learners to explore different sorts of questions that expand transformative and liberatory engagement within and beyond the classroom. For example, beyond simply providing a list of "mental health" resources, learning communities can think critically about the ways in which mental states are inseparable from broader systems of power and oppression: How are widespread depression and anxiety cultivated under White supremacist, cisheteropatriarchal, capitalism (Cvetkovich, 2012)? How do oppressive systems and social structures inflict traumatic harm against all people in ways that normalize particular mental/emotional states, especially for marginalized and oppressed folk (Barlow, 2018)? Furthermore, how are currently offered "mental health" resources entangled with systems of dominance (Berila, 2016)? Are colleges and universities providing these resources in an effort to avoid meaningfully addressing other issues, such as the colonization of Indigenous lands, the spread of anti-Asian hate, and the pervasive antiblackness which has forever shaped the history of higher education? Raising Mad questions like these is necessary for identifying how sanism operates to undermine critical thinking/resistance. In other words, how sanism obscures power through a focus on what is "wrong" with individual people.

Part of what I am arguing here is that the mental and emotional states of students are not just external to the classroom, and they cannot just be sent elsewhere for support as that is an act of irresponsibility on the part of educators. If we are truly determined to realize a vision of "education as the practice of freedom," then our interactions and conversations with students must move beyond the limitation of pathology, particularly when our classes broach topics of oppression that are traumatic or emotionally challenging. I am not advocating that educators pretend to be therapists or that a classroom is a good location for therapy, but we simply cannot teach toward freedom if students are not free to experience and express the wholeness of their being. Sometimes that means crying or getting into a heated debate or stimming. It can also mean that students need access to different ways of being present/not present in the classroom. For example, in my online classes, I often give students an option to disengage from discussion boards and submit an alternative confidential assignment on weeks that feel overly personal or emotionally challenging for them. I also accept multiple formats of engagement on the discussion boards, which can include drawings, songs, stories—anything, really, so long as it demonstrates their engagement with the learning materials. I strive to honor their wholeness by giving them power to control their engagement with the learning materials for the class.

Moreover, practicing anti-sanist teaching means that social justice educators must deliberately seek to build and sustain solidarity with Mad peoples and communities in anti-sanist struggles. Similar to how abolitionist teaching cannot be isolated from the lived experiences and needs of communities of color (Love, 2019) and how feminist teaching is indivisible from social movements against gendered violence/oppression (Shrewsbury, 1993), Mad pedagogies aim to practice alliance with peoples who have been most impacted by sanist institutions/belief systems, and that core alliance is the guiding impetus for education. Teaching from Mad solidarity means, in part, actively challenging sanism as it manifests in learning spaces and encouraging students to cultivate a habit of doing the same. It also means teaching in ways that support students in critically reflection about their own relationships to Madness without shame or judgment. It also means teaching in ways that get students into their own habits of solidarity with Mad peoples and communities, whether through building community connections, language, and/or empathy.

Doing these things opens space for students to practice solidarity with other social movements as well because sanism is indivisible from other systems/structures of power (Diamond, 2013). Consequently, reimagining social justice education through anti-sanism is not about decentering race, class, gender, etc. but rather is a method for making teaching about power and oppression more nuanced, inclusive, equitable, and just. Time spent discussing sanism is also spent discussing racism, classism, sexism, and so on, for systems/structures of dominance are not mutually exclusive, but rather interdependent. In addition, discussing sanism actually creates space for teachers and students to think critically about the outcomes of White Supremacy, capitalism, and cis-heteropatriarchy which too often get overlooked or marginalized, such as how medical models of mental "health"/mental "illness" are socially constructed to obscure the psychic impacts of power and oppression (Barlow, 2018; Cvetkovich, 2012; Snyder et al., 2019). Developing a sustained, substantive critique of sanism is a meaningful tool for teaching against multiple, intersecting systems of dominance that generates necessary space for the expression of mental and emotional difference, and it also provides an entry point for thinking about how social justice is simultaneously an internal and external process.

Practicing Anti-Sanism in Education

So, given the importance of practicing social justice education through an anti-sanist commitment to collective access and liberation, we must then ask ourselves, "Which aspects of social justice education must evolve or be transformed in order for educators and learners to consciously resist sanism and to promote Mad liberation?" We must recommit to intersectionality and an ecological analysis of systems of oppression (Levins Morales, 1998), and we must also question how our practices of intersectionality have become stifled, leading us to center particular marginalized peoples while neglecting or excluding others. To answer these questions and fulfill these commitments, we have to be willing to acknowledge our own limitations and seek to become ever better versions of ourselves. For me, questioning where intersectionality gets stifled is particularly important because rather than using this framework as a tool to understand the complexity and dynamic nature of power, it often gets limited to studying a different location with the "matrix of domination" (Collins, 1990). As a result, instead of developing a habit of reflexivity and humility, people claiming intersectionality are often unwilling to explore additional and/or alternative perspectives to their own. Anti-sanist practice provides an opportunity to get out of such ruts.

What does anti-sanism look like in practice for social justice educators? I argue it encompasses many of the same tenets of transformative justice, and also more. Transformative justice is an anti-carceral, community-based approach to resisting harm that prioritizes accountability, relationship building, and collective action (Mingus, 2019; Dixon & Piepzna-Samarasinha, 2020). It situates moments of violence and harm within broader social arrangements in an effort to understand why people acted the way they did, how they were impacted, and what needs to change to prevent harms from occurring again. In terms of solidarity with Mad people, transformative justice in the classroom entails making an effort to understand how nearly all learning spaces, including social justice learning spaces, are formed against the experiences and needs of Mad/neurodiverse/neuroqueer students. And, from that understanding, collaboratively working to create space for neurodiversity, different mental states, and different forms of enmindedment through ongoing resistance to sanism and "compulsory able-mindedness" (Kafer, 2013). This task can be particularly difficult in academia, which is built on sanist notions of intelligence, rationality, and elitism, but it is also especially viral for this same reason.

Refusing sanism in our teaching also likely entails shifting how we approach other forms of oppression and how we endeavor to stimulate, promote, and deepen students' critical consciousness. For example, centering conversations around the "medical industrial complex" (Mingus, 2015), especially aspects of it which are connected to "mental health" and "mental illness," is a good place to start because it gives students the opportunity to intentionally reflect on where ideas about mental and emotional difference come from and how they are socially, historically, and politically grounded. Talking about the medical industrial complex creates space for conversations about how medicalization and pathologization have been used against multiple oppressed communities, whether in terms of sexual and domestic violence (Durazo, 2006), slavery and incarceration (Meerai et al., 2016), or other enactments of dominance. Additionally, naming and critiquing the medical-industrial complex shifts the conversation away from what is "wrong" with particular students toward how social institutions function to create ideas of normalcy in order to regulate how people express themselves and their needs. From this shift can emerge critical conversations about how to build different kinds of relationships that make space for people to exist as they are and how we can all better respond to one another's access needs.

One particularly important way that anti-sanist teaching might transform social justice education is by establishing greater opportunities for cross-movement solidarity, for sanism is one of the bridges that unites different systems of power. Some examples of what this cross-movement solidarity might look like include:

* Furthering critiques of respectability politics by demonstrating how they have been utilized to normalize particular forms of enmindedment which surveil, regulate, and discipline oppressed peoples.
* Moving away from individual or cultural explanations for "mental illness" in order to identify the lingering psychic impacts of oppression, both on those shouldering the burden of it as well as those who benefit from it.
* Generating empathy through a deeper understanding of experiences, and especially through an awareness of the interconnectedness of lived experiences—for example, how the suicidality and self-harm of queer and trans* folks is connected to the harm of an imposed gender binary.
* Examining how the tactic of pathologization has been used across systems of power, in ways that are unique but clearly interwoven, to press people to access oppressive realities and/or to punish them for calling for accountability from more advantaged subjects.

At the foundation of cross-movement solidarity is the idea that struggles against power and oppression are not mutually exclusive; we can share in one another's struggles and care for one another without losing sight of our own experiences and needs. The result of doing so is that we build bridges to each other that can sustain and unite us. In terms of education, teaching toward cross-movement solidarity from an anti-sanist position empowers students and teachers alike to exceed boundaries and to better recognize how similar forces co-operate across sites of difference. Thinking critically about medicalization and pathologization gives us tools for collaboration and empathy. Moreover, seeking out ways to overcome deficit thinking by instead understanding the psychic impacts of oppression is a way of developing genuine empathy and understanding from which we can forge different ways of being together that are more just.

Note

1 My use of ecological here is informed by the work of Aurora Levins Morales (1998), who argues that social justice work must be holistic given that struggles against power are always deeply interconnected (i.e., they form ecosystems of oppression). The term resonates with me and my work because it centers interdependence, solidarity, and collective resistance, all of which are vital components of the disability justice framework that guides my thinking (Mingus, 2017; Sins Invalid, 2016).

References

Balén, J. (2005). Practicing what we teach. In E. Lapovsky Kennedy & A. Beins (Eds.), *Women's Studies for the Future: Foundations, Interrogations, Politics* (pp. 272–284). Rutgers.

Barlow, J. N. (2018). Resorting optimal Black mental health and reversing intergenerational trauma in an era of Black Lives Matter. *Biography, 41*(4), 895–908.

Ben-Moshe, L., & Carey, A. (2014). *Disability incarcerated: Imprisonment and disability in the United States and Canada.* Palgrave Macmillan.

Berila, B. (2016). Mindfulness as a healing, liberatory practice in queer anti-oppression pedagogy. *Social Alternatives, 25*(3), 5–10.

Brueck, J., & McNeill, Z. Z. (2020). *Queer and trans voices: Achieving liberation through consistent anti-oppression.* Sanctuary Publishers.

Collins, P. H. (1990). *Black feminist thought: Knowledge, consciousness, and the politics of empowerment.* Routledge.

Cvetkovich, A. (2012). Depression is ordinary: Public feelings and Saidiya Hartman's lose your mother. *Feminist Theory, 13*(2), 131–146.

Diamond, S. (2013). What makes us a community? Reflections on building solidarity in anti-sanist praxis. In B. A. LeFrançois, R. Menzies, & G. Reaume (Eds.), *Mad matters: A critical reader in Canadian Mad Studies* (pp. 64–78). Canadian Scholars' Press.

Durazo, A. C. R. (2006). Medical violence against people of color and the medicalization of domestic violence. In Incite! Women of Color Against Violence (Ed.), *Color of Violence: The Incite! Anthology* (pp. 179–190). Duke University Press.

Dixon, E. & Piepzna-Samarasinha, L. L. (Eds.). (2020). *Beyond survival: Strategies and stories from the transformative justice movement.* AK Press.

hooks, b. (1994). *Teaching to transgress: Education as the practice of freedom.* Routledge.

Jordan, J. (1992). *Technical difficulties: African-American notes on the state of the union.* Pantheon Books.

Kafer, A. (2013). *Feminist, queer, crip.* Indiana University Press.

Levins Morales, A. (1998). *Medicine stories: History, culture and the politics of integrity.* South End Press.

Lorde, A., & Hall, J. W. (2004). *Conversations with Audre Lorde.* University Press of Mississippi.

Love, B. (2019). *We want to do more than survive: Abolitionist teaching and the pursuit of educational freedom.* Beacon Press.

Maines, R. (2014). Socially camouflaged technologies: The case of the electromechanical vibrator. In M. Wyer, M. Barbercheck, D. Cookmeyer, Ö. Öztürk, and M. Wayne (Eds.), *Women, science, and technology: A reader in feminist science studies.* Routledge.

Meerai, S., Abdillahi, I., and Poole, J. (2016). An introduction to anti-Black Sanism. *Intersectionalities: A Global Journal of Social Work Analysis, Research, Polity, and Practice,* 5(3).

Menzies, R. J., Reaume, G., & LeFrançois, B. A. (2013). *Mad matters: A critical reader in Canadian mad studies.* Canadian Scholars' Press.

Mingus, M. (2015). Medical industrial complex visual. *Leaving Evidence.* https://leavingevidence.wordpress.com/2015/02/06/medical-industrial-complex-visual/ (published February 6, 2015).

Mingus, M. (2019). Access intimacy, interdependence and disability justice. Retrieved from *Leaving Evidence.* https://leavingevidence.wordpress.com/2017/04/12/access-intimacy-interdependence-and-disability-justice/ (published April 12, 2017).

Redikopp, S. (2021). Out of place, out of mind: Min(d)ing race in mad studies through a metaphor of spatiality. *Canadian Journal of Disability Studies,* 10(3), 96–118.

Sensoy, Ö., & DiAngelo, R. (2014). Respect differences? Challenging the common guidelines in social justice education. *Democracy & Education,* 22(2), 1–10.

Shrewsbury, C. (1997 [1993]). What is feminist pedagogy?. *Women's Studies Quarterly,* 25(1/2), 166–173.

Sins Invalid. (2016). Skin, tooth, and bone. The basis of movement is our people: A disability justice primer. *Sins Invalid.*

Snyder, S., Pitt, K.-A., Shanouda, F., Voronka, J., Reid, J., & Landry, D. (2019). Unlearning through mad studies: Disruptive pedagogical praxis. *Curriculum Inquiry,* 49(4), 485–502.

Spade. D. (2006). Multilating Gender. In S. Stryker & S. Whittle (Eds.), *The transgender studies reader* (pp. 315–332). Routledge.

Starkman, M. (2013). The movement. In B. A. LeFrançois, R. Menzies, & G. Reaume (Eds.), *Mad matters: A critical reader in Canadian mad studies* (pp. 27–37). Canadian Scholars' Press.

Taylor, A., & Hunt-Hendrix, L. (2019). One for all: To avert global catastrophe, we urgently need to resurrect the ancient ideal of solidarity. *The New Republic.* https://newrepublic.com/article/154623/green-new-deal-solidarity-solution-climate-change-global-warming (published August 26, 2019).

Ussher, J. (2013). Diagnosing difficult women and pathologizing femininity: Gender bias in psychiatric nosology. *Feminism and Psychology,* 23(1), 63–69.

· 12 ·

THE HEGEMONY IN THE ROOM

Phillip A. Boda

I end this work not as a finality of benchmarks or by expressing coming to terms with how the world has been made and how we interpret it. Instead, I leave the reader with a musing and poem I wrote when reading through the works for this volume, thinking about my own research as a critical scholar working in education. And as we embark on our next steps toward exploring the educational injustices among margins and centers, we must also engage our Selves—those many facets of Self that perform specific cultural markers in specific contexts—in ways that does more than merely deconstruct that which has already occurred, and instead offers a new path forward. It is with the words of the eminent Audre Lorde that I encourage you to hold space for how we can pursue new futures of education where margins and centers no longer are prevalent or home.

> Within the interdependence of mutual (nondominant) differences lies that security which enables us to descend into the chaos of knowledge and return with true visions of our future, along with the concomitant power to effect those changes which can bring that future into being ... those of us who have been forged in the crucibles of difference—those of us who are poor, who are lesbians, who are Black, who are older—know that survival is not an academic skill. It is learning how to take our differences and make them strengths. For the master's tools will never dismantle the master's house. They may allow us temporarily to beat him at his own game, but they will never enable us to bring about genuine change. (Lorde, 1984, p. 111)

Taking Audre Lorde's eminent quote seriously means that all systems and subjectivities that have continually sustained cultures of oppression who, by their very purpose, were meant to subjugate must be first deconstructed to explore their making: We must expose perceptions of normalcy as "ideological or culturally constructed rather than as nature or a simple reflection of reality" (Collins, 1991, p. 14). In doing so, we encourage radical sociocultural readings of these norms to disrupt the political alignments and pedagogical qualities that maintain these cultural affiliations as the normative center from which all things are measured. *We write into existence that we Matter.*

For those in education, we recognize the need for such a critical turn as the power of this work has been striving to take hold and flourish since Paulo Freire's first English translation of *Pedagogy of the oppressed* (1970), fifty years ago, as well as 30+ years since the seminal work by Patricia Hill Collins, *Black feminist thought*, and Audre Lorde's, *Sister outsider*. Deconstruction is just the start, though. In their place, we must cultivate and sustain systems and subjectivities that *counter-narrate, resist marginalization*, and *foster growth* (Anzaldúa, 1987) emphasizing that this dialectic praxis is always negotiated. Such work disrupts hegemony that valorizes predatory "winner-takes-all" ideological commitments, whose "best bang for your buck" approach seeks only to maintain the normative center that purposes the Margins as disposable. Such utilitarian ethics of value-added impact makes those subject to Discursive, psychic, and physical violence even more so, while denying the precarious effects of such choices. *We know this, and we demand that we Matter.*

This volume, therefore, sought a coalition of diverse, unsettled cases, musings, and theorizations in education to dismantle this systemic stronghold of oppressive hegemony that pinnacles individual utility with no obligation to community relevance. We trouble the binary between individual and community—between Self/Other (Schalk, 2011)—to show how scholars developed nuanced relational ways of understanding notions of justice, equity, and the purpose of education: To open up paths for unknown futures to take hold and for new visions of what criticality means for schools, agency, and personhood: *As We Gaze Deeply Toward Dismantlement and Liberation.*

WE HOPE YOU GAZE WITH US. It reminds me of cold butter

> Not in substantive quality, but in consistency
> That slippery feeling—Untenable
> Massively known as there, but also not
> Similar to
>   And no less symbolic of
> Textures embodied in words and the world
> Undeniable, yet fictive in materiality
>   but no less impactful
> as a knife slips through cold butter

THE HEGEMONY IN THE ROOM

Almost as if the knife
Which is used to fillet this perceived
    stabilized entity
Is rather, instead, engulfed in a texture
In this process of engagement

Fathomable—yet, Untenable
    not impossibly seen, heard, or felt

Cutting through cold butter with a sharp piece of metal figures an interaction
And also
A state of action
Both bold, yet reserved

In a sense, so too are words
And our world
Shaped and shaded
Through milieu
    With and enmeshed among the mythic social qualities that breach our bodies,
    hearts, and   souls—At every turn

Our Eyes, bodies, hearts, and spirits
Negotiating
Place, Space
    Time

This expressive work—as it were
    To gesticulate in ways
Making evident a substance
That speaks with and through this act
    A seemingly rote engagement With our Selves, and Others

Yet
Often described as
    Moot of Our Selves
    Of Our Dreams
Denying any and all freedom beyond
    The Story told about Us, Without Us—Figured "Above" Us

So, in this interaction
Of physical
Of emotive
Of spiritual
Poiesis

Of becoming
We refuse to accept the articulated impossible
Which binds our Eyes-bodies-minds-spirits
Enforcing single-state conjectures of what is—Of who is "what," and why

We learn to expect resistance
Like that of a knife cutting through cold butter
To read the word and the world
Through both our Beings
And those embodiments
Of stories
    Passed on
Demanding a focus, Discarding a presence
Of histories past
Of/In histories present
And through just futures

But that makes this work no less tenable
    Rather, its presence is ([re]made) self-evident
At every turn
At every (re)cognition
At every maneuver
Used to expose the cracks
    Broken and seething
From the blood, sweat, and souls
    Of those that walk with Us/before Us/among Us/through Us

And yet
When we suggest: We Matter
That Our experiences
Are not merely
Anecdotes of individuated constitution
That as we bring fire to this stage
We pursue our Lives Beyond Recognition
    To Bear Witness to our Experiences
    Our Souls
    As greater than the sum of our Ancestors' Wildest Dreams

To Not be beyond respect
To Not be beyond value
To bear witness
To that which
    In rooms blooming with Life
That our Selves

Our Lives
Our Love
Our Souls . . . Matter

And as we refuse
To dampen our Light
We pass the Fire on
Born and Bred
In spaces
    Tenable
        And filled with Joy, Love, Compassion, Breath!

Knowing all along
That butter is only slippery when cold
    Muted
Denied exposure to Warmth

And that We, as Lived Beings
    See
        Feel
            Hold Close
Those precious forms of activity
That reveal
How words
And the World
Are sutured
    In the face of hemorrhaging Eyes, bodies, hearts, and souls

And still
    We Rise
Not to the occasion, but to Replete our hi/her/their(stories)
    With narratives anew
    Built with one purpose: To tell the world, We Matter

We Matter
In ways unknown to that thick, cold anemia of
    The "World"
In ways untouched by its sharp fictions
    That story our Eyes, bodies, hearts, and souls as dispensable
    Disposable
        Devoid of Centering

We Demand We Matter

In rejoice to the warming of that interactive joining between material and immaterial
    Laid bare naked
    Judged by all
    Our Contours—Our Scrapes—Our Aggressions
That have been, and continue to be,
    Noted as exceptions to the rule

That we focus on the warmth
    The derivative stories not yet told
About Eyes, bodies, hearts, and souls
    Indispensable
Satiates this once thick milieu
    devoid of gentleness
And then we see what that feeling was/is all along

A Fictive Voice
A Sutured Wound
A Hurting Soul

Beyond those unquestionable actions that are unforgiveable
    We find Peace
    We support Love
    We Demand that We Matter

And in the end,
When Flowers and Hearts bloom where once there was shivering exile and a solemn vacuum
The Hegemony in the Room
    Can be reckoned with
    Can be relieved of its purpose, for a new path forward: To Heal.

References

Anzaldúa, G. (1987). *Borderlands/La Frontera: The new mestiza*. Aunt Lute Book Company.
Collins, P. H. (1991). *Black feminist thought: Knowledge, consciousness, and the politics of empowerment*. Routledge.
Freire, P. (1970). *Pedagogy of the oppressed* (M. B. Ramos, Trans.). Continuum.
Lorde, A. (1984). *Sister outsider: Essays and speeches*. Crossing Press.
Schalk, S. (2011). Self, other and other-self: Going beyond the self/other binary in contemporary consciousness. *Journal of Comparative Research in Anthropology and Sociology, 2*, 197–210.

Studies in Criticality

General Editor
Shirley R. Steinberg

Counterpoints publishes the most compelling and imaginative books being written in education today. Grounded on the theoretical advances in criticalism, feminism, and postmodernism in the last two decades of the twentieth century, Counterpoints engages the meaning of these innovations in various forms of educational expression. Committed to the proposition that theoretical literature should be accessible to a variety of audiences, the series insists that its authors avoid esoteric and jargonistic languages that transform educational scholarship into an elite discourse for the initiated. Scholarly work matters only to the degree it affects consciousness and practice at multiple sites. Counterpoints' editorial policy is based on these principles and the ability of scholars to break new ground, to open new conversations, to go where educators have never gone before.

For additional information about this series or for the submission of manuscripts, please contact:

> Shirley R. Steinberg, General Editor
> msgramsci@gmail.com

To order other books in this series, please contact our Customer Service Department:

> peterlang@presswarehouse.com (within the U.S.)
> orders@peterlang.com (outside the U.S.)

Or browse online by series:

> www.peterlang.com

www.ingramcontent.com/pod-product-compliance
Lightning Source LLC
Chambersburg PA
CBHW061718300426
44115CB00014B/2741